BARELY BREATHING

A MEMOIR

MICHAEL PETERSON

Cover Design and Interior Layout by
Ellie Bockert Augsburger
Creative Digital Studios
www.creativedigitalstudios.com

Editing Services provided by
Delano Amiel
Creative Digital Studios
www.creativedigitalstudios.com

Cover Design Features

Water droplets on a glass surface
© Dmitry Shishov / Dollar Photo Club

Salzburg city on sunset with castle view, Austria
© Freesurf / Dollar Photo Club

To Ethan and Christian.

This book is dedicated to you. I hope that you find your way in your journey and that you reach a place where it all makes sense. I love you both immeasurably.

To Wendy

You threw a drowning man a life preserver and you saved me in every possible way. This book would have never become a reality if not for the love, passion and inspiration you gave. You awoke something that was dormant and lost deep inside of me. You made me feel again. You made me love again. You made me believe again. My feelings for you will last forever. IWALU ICHI.

*"I'm falling apart.
I'm barely breathing.
With a broken heart.
That's still beating.
In the pain, there is healing.
In your name, I find meaning."*

-Lyrics from Broken, by Lifehouse

FOREWORD

I was frantically running through the crowded streets of Salzburg, Austria in the blazing mid-day heat of a late-July scorcher. My vision was becoming cloudy through a growing swell of sweat and tears, I was panicked. I had been traveling for thirty hours straight and hadn't slept at all in three days. I didn't know if Dad had died alone scared in the night or if he was holding on; waiting for me, waiting to die. The image was haunting and drove me to get to him.

I didn't know exactly where the hospital was. I had gotten vague directions from a cab driver in broken English and the bus drivers were no help. I was openly praying to God (whose very existence I questioned) that I could get to him in time. "Please don't let him die", I said as my tears mixed with my sweat and burnt a path across my cheeks "Please don't let him die alone!"

I had to get to him, I knew he was scared. The doctors called and told us that he probably wasn't going to make it through the night. They said if any family member was going to get there, it had to be now. More than a day had gone by since I got that message and left my home in Boulder, Colorado. I didn't know if he was still alive or if he was already dead but I was running as fast as I could. Although I was running towards him, I was also running away. I was running away from my own deteriorating life, my own fears and my own fragmented faith.

The sweat was pouring off of me, and my legs burned in pain. I yearned for rest, but I had to press on. As I struggled, key moments of my life with my Dad were flashing before me. The memories flowed through my mind like a silent movie on fast forward, reminding me of the times he encouraged me when I was defeated and how he helped me find my way when I was lost. If only he was here to help me now. I was lost and I needed to find him; I was lost and I needed to find me.

My struggle to find my way in my own life and my need for meaning collided with my emotional surrender to my Dad and the need to be there for him in the final moments of his life. Somewhere in the streets of Salzburg and beyond, I lost my Dad but I found something in myself that I had been searching for as long as I can remember.

The times that I shared with my Dad in his final days were some of the most important moments of my life. It wasn't what I always thought it would be but it was poignant and meaningful in its own way and I will never forget it. It was gut-wrenchingly painful to say goodbye to him, knowing it would be the last time that I would ever see him. The circumstances of his death were dramatic and excruciating. They took me on a physical, emotional and spiritual journey that I was not ready for; a journey that changed who I am and how I view my life.

It gives me a great sense of peace and pride to know that I was there for him. As difficult as it was, I was the one who moved earth and sky to fulfill his final wish. I was the one who had to tell him he would never leave that foreign hospital alive. It was me who presented and discussed his options with him, even though I knew he had none. I was the one who gave him a strong shoulder to lean on in his darkest hours when the demons came; when he was weakened and needed someone to carry him, I was there. I will never forget it. It was incredibly difficult, heartbreaking, exhausting and rewarding at the same time. My Dad's death probably changed me in ways that I still haven't realized.

The relationship between a father and son is a multi-layered, typically unclear thing that I was able to reflect on and experience in a unique way with my own Dad over the last 10 days of his life. For anyone that has lost a parent, more specifically a son that lost his father, you understand how life altering it can be. You find yourself questioning your life and ultimately your faith, it changes you. It leaves you feeling vulnerable and truly alone. I found myself reaching for the phone for months after Dad was gone, only to realize each time that there was no one to call. It is as if the last piece of your childhood goes with him and there is a void left where he used to be. All of a sudden, there is no one to rescue you; no one to lean on when times get tough and no one to draw strength from like you could from him.

Now that it is my privilege to provide that strength and guidance to my own children, I can see the profound and unconditional love they have for me in their eyes. I also see the vulnerability they have to me and I realize that I had the same vulnerability to my Dad. He helped me prepare for my own journey without even knowing it, just by loving me and being who he was; flaws included. I miss him and I miss sharing my life with him. It may sound cliché' to say it but he was more than my Dad, he was also my friend.

For a few years after Dad was gone, people would hear my story and they would be over-whelmed by it. "That is an unbelievable story. You should write a book about it, it's heart-breaking!" they would unanimously say. I never really seriously considered it and thought it might come off as too self-indulgent or self-important. Why would anyone care about my story about my Dad's final days? Why would anyone care about my bond with my Dad and how painful it was to lose him, or the extreme circumstances surrounding his death and how it helped me find my-self? I told the story from time to time and was always amazed and a little touched by how people reacted to it. As this dialogue repeated itself over and over again through the years, I started to consider writing a book more and more.

Everyone who has lost a father can relate. Everyone who lost someone special can relate. Everyone who struggles with questions of faith can relate and even those fortunate enough to have found faith can relate. This accounts for just about everyone. Anyone who has ever experienced a loved one's death and searched for absolution, truth, faith, compassion and personal healing can relate.

I have been on a journey of my own since long before my father died. I guess you would call it your run-of-the-mill spiritual quest for truth and enlightenment. For most of my adult life, I have been in search of answers to the great questions that have challenged all of mankind. Why are we here? Is there something higher than us out there? Do we have souls? Does consciousness survive death? Will Mom and Dad be there when I die? Why can't I ever hear, see or feel them since they died? Are they here? Are they watching over me?

I consider myself spiritual but not religious, which is an easy and classic pretext from the responsibilities and corruption of modern day religion. I like my Sundays free and I don't like guilt. I consider myself a Christian but I am scared to commit. I am scared for many reasons but mainly because I am not sure what is really out there. I don't know what is real from what is imagined. I am scared about death and the prospect of the "beyond". I'm scared of not being. Most of all, I'm scared of not feeling.

Like a lot of people, I have always been more of a goal seeker than a journey lover. This to a fault typifies me and most of the first forty years of my life. Every now and then I wake up and lay in bed, I think about my life and I realize that I honestly can't remember most of the last twenty years. There are little bits and pieces and fragmented parts, but I can't always remember every-thing and I can't always remember being. I wonder to myself, where is the meaning in this? Can this be all that there is? Shouldn't there be more? It makes me feel like I am missing something – something critical about my life and its purpose.

Sometimes it feels as though I am idly staggering through life and that it's all going too fast. I wake up every day and simply do what needs to be done; Work, kids, marriage, sleep, etc., over and over and over. After each day another arrives and then fades away like its predecessor. There is no ceremony. There is no anthem. There is no audience. There is just the inevitability of time passing with no way to stop it, not even for a second. The days turn into weeks; the weeks turn into months; the months turn into years, and before I realized it, my life was not what it was supposed to be.

I have been driven most of my adult life by an intense fear of failure that sometimes pushes me to extremes. I tend to be focused on the next goal, to get to the next attainment level whether it's personal or professional. I spend my time striving for success rather than living and loving the journey because I am afraid of not attaining. I'm afraid of failing. The problem with this, of course, is waking up someday and realizing that your life has passed you by and it's almost too late to start living. You want to start, you really do. But you don't know how.

What does it take to wake us up? Is it ever too late to start living? Every so often when I have a moment of introspection I reconcile myself to stop and smell the roses, to seize the day and to hang on to any other cliché I can find. Then I wake up the next day and get lost again in work and kids and the malaise of life for months at a time.

I think there are a lot of people like me out there. I guess you might say that it's a classic mid-life crisis.

*****

I grew up middle class and was raised as a traditional Catholic in a very nice, insulated private school in Harrisburg, Pennsylvania. I was the youngest of the family with two older brothers, Danny and Rich and one older sister, Janet. Danny was two years older than me and as the middle child waged epic battles between both me and our brother Rich, who was two years older than Danny. Janet was the oldest and was eight years older than me. She was the mentoring big sister to all of us and a particularly good sport when we would gang up and torture her over the years. She was a saint and we were little devils.

We didn't have a lot of money, but we never needed anything. By all measures, it was a privileged childhood, not decadent or spoiled, but privileged. In Catholic school, I was taught that everything the Church says, teaches and preaches is simple fact. Everyone else is wrong and is destined to burn in hell. It all seemed so absolute and had no gray areas at all. All throughout my schooling and religious teachings, I always had my doubts and reservations. As I grew older and shook off the institutional guilt of free thinking as well as copious amounts of free touching, I began to explore my own spirituality to try to answer the questions of life and faith and meaning for myself. You could say I became your typical recovering Catholic.

The obvious hypocrisy of the Catholic Church and its history is hard for anyone who truly approaches things with an open mind to ignore. I realized it was important to figure things out for myself rather than just taking their word for it. I wanted to believe that Jesus turned water into wine; I wanted to believe that Mary conceived as a virgin; I wanted to believe that a flesh and bone man rose from the dead after three days, and I wanted to believe all of the stories I was taught as fact. Unfortunately, I also felt like I would really benefit from a little proof. A little incontrovertible evidence would be nice. Like many jaded, cynical people in modern times, I became a classic "doubting Thomas". However, there was always something there, gnawing away at me, that told me it was all real.

For years, my urge to search for a hint of spiritual enlightenment would come and go with the ebb and flow of life. It's not necessarily something I think about very often, but it's always there waiting for me; like that nagging feeling that you left the stove on, or wondering if you accidentally locked the cats in a room without food and water while you take a two day business trip.

Every now and then when the music of my life pauses, I find time between songs to continue my search. This search has led me down many paths with different schools of thought. I have read philosophies on the world's religions. There are many synergies among them, but no real answers and of course, no proof. There is only an overriding need for something that has been fleeting around me for most of my life. Faith.

I have seen regression hypnotists with the express purpose of trying to attain some name, place or historical fact that I could verify to be real and not just a figment of my imagination. Through it all, I had interesting experiences but I found none of the factual experience I sought.

I have channeled mediums to reach Mom and Dad in the great beyond and was exposed to shysters and con artists. I paid one crackpot two hundred dollars to channel the "light beings" who speak to him, he told me nothing he couldn't get from my questionnaire. I have even investigated witchcraft and Ouija boards but found only fear and darkness. I was looking anywhere and everywhere to find answers and proof to my very basic questions about faith, but I was coming up empty handed each time. Still, I kept searching.

I was in an empty and loveless marriage that was falling apart after 14 years of dysfunction and loneliness. I had been living in the basement for a year and had given up on my relationship; I was beginning to stray in every way possible. I was silently hoping and praying for a return of passion into my life. I was dying inside and I knew my marriage was all but over.

My wife Megan and I didn't love each other anymore. I am not sure that we ever did. Certainly not in the way I wanted or the way I dreamed about when I contemplated it in my younger years. It never felt like we had a completely emotional, physical or spiritual surrender to each other. I see now that Megan just wasn't capable of that in the way I needed. Her lack of identity, her narcissism and her depression were a lethal combination that made her miserable and left us both empty, lonely and unsatisfied for most of our time together. Over the years, I found solace in anything and everything that avoided what we both knew to be true.

Megan had a huge hole in her brought on by years of abuse and neglect at the hands of a cruel, sinister, alcoholic father. I wanted to be the one to change her but I failed miserably. I guess I wanted to save her when I asked her to marry me. It felt good at the time but I always had a voice inside telling me that something wasn't right. Looking back now, I can see that we were wrong for each other in every way imaginable. As our marriage was nearing its end, we both felt angry, broken, ashamed, desperate and scared. My experience with Megan has proven to me without a doubt that you can't truly love someone if you don't love yourself first. In all the years I knew her, Megan could never even look at herself in the mirror.

As the years passed, I realized that the emptiness inside of her was something I could never fill. As was often the case, over time I became the focus and cause of her discontent. Nothing was ever good enough. The nicest house on the block wasn't enough. Lots of money wasn't enough. Two beautiful children weren't enough. No matter what I did, I couldn't fill the emptiness she felt. As her resentment and misery grew year after year, I grew tired of taking the blame for it. My need for passion, love and intimacy led me to someone else and to living with the spiders in the basement. Still, the decision to split and leave the kids was something I was struggling with greatly. There is very little pain like the pain you feel on the day you move out on your young children.

I was a reasonably successful workaholic and was supremely devoted to my two boys. My sons, Ethan and Christian mean everything to me. Feeling the connection to them on a level that is beyond flesh and bone showed me some of the faith that I had been searching for in every nook and cranny of life, however it gave me none of the answers I sought. Through it all, I continued to ponder the great beyond, my place in it and what it all meant to me and for my life.

So there I was, free-falling into my mid-life crisis with no brakes. I was lost in my career and had become a typical working-class drone trying to climb the corporate ladder by working twenty-four seven. My marriage was dead. I was falling in love with someone else which brought tremendous feelings of guilt, exhilaration, desire and shame. I couldn't find my faith. I couldn't tell you when I lost it or where it went or if I ever really, truly had it. I didn't know what I believed anymore. I didn't know who I was anymore. I was officially lost.

Then everything changed.

My dad's death and everything that came with it has led me to some places of emotional pain and exhaustion, financial hardship, intense introspection; lost and ultimately found self and faith.

These events have also led me to a place filled with more hope, peace and understanding. They have led me to a place where I am comfortable without having all of the answers, and it has led to a renewed understanding of what is most important in life – to me.

I think it can be different for everyone. Like the character Curly from the movie City Slickers put it so perfectly, "The secret to life is just one thing," as he held his finger up in the air. He went on to explain to Billy Crystal's character Mitch that it is something that each person needs to figure out for themselves. I know it is a made up line from a Hollywood movie but it touched me the first time I saw it. Now as I come out the backside of this epic journey of loss and search for meaning, I am more drawn to it. It has wisdom and I am certain now that I know what that "one thing" is. It gives me hope.

The journey that my Dad's dramatic ending took me on and my role in it was the catalyst for me to find my "one thing." For years beyond my Dad's death and even to today, I continue to ponder it. But I have found a peacefulness and understanding that has made my life better. Life is not perfect and it is certainly not what I dreamed it would be. Like anyone else, there are peaks and valleys in my life and sometimes real pain too.

As I took on the task of writing my Dad's Eulogy, which is easily one of the most difficult, heart-wrenching, soul-searching, yet rewarding things I have ever done. I felt a tremendous pressure. How do you do justice to someone who has been everything to you and for you, for your entire existence? How do you properly honor them and say "Thank You" or "Good-bye" in a way that encapsulates who they were, what they did for you and what they meant to you? It is a tall order, indeed. To this day, I still choke up a little when I read his Eulogy. I hope he heard it. I hope he liked it. I hope I nailed it. I hope he is proud of me.

When you're in the fog of your life sometimes you can only see the fog. If you somehow manage to get above it, you still see the fog but eventually it burns off and you can see through it. You can see things you didn't notice before. Things start to take shape and make sense. You see things from a different perspective.

So after having a few years to let the fog clear and reflecting on this experience that still seems like yesterday to me, I realize its significance in understanding what my "one thing" is. I now know that my story can be everyone's story. The names and places are different. The circumstances are different. The dynamics of the relationship are different but fundamentally, we all experience loss and we all face the same questions of meaning, inevitability, purpose and faith. We all are in search of our "one thing."

If my story of the toughest and most meaningful parts of my life can touch anyone and help them find the meaning that eludes so many of us, then I will always be willing to tell it. So I decided to write a book about it.

This is my story. This is about finding meaning in the

face of heartbreaking loss.

This is about my Dad.

"Something is about to give.
I can feel it coming.
I think I know what it is.
I'm not afraid to die
I'm not afraid to live
And when I'm flat on my back
I hope to feel like I did"

- Lyrics from Kite, by U2

CHAPTER 1

The Little League World Series is the largest youth sports tournament in the world. Every year, teams from forty-seven countries work to reach the pinnacle of their little league baseball dreams. An international tournament that ends in Williamsport, Pennsylvania each August that crowns district champions, state champions, regional champions and ultimately, a World Champion. Amidst the triumphs and heartbreaks, hopes and dreams are either realized or lost. It is a celebration of community, childhood and everything that is great about baseball and youth sports. It is America at its finest.

In many ways, shapes and forms, childhood events like this are metaphors for life and for the relationships that mean the most to us.

I am particularly cognizant of how youth sports can be the foundation that determines the kind of men and women our children can become. As a coach of many youth sports teams, I uphold this belief in my interactions with my players and their parents. Each game, each pass, each pitch, each lap, each vault, each individual inning, quarter, meet and contest is an opportunity for personal growth and the formation of building blocks of individuality for each kid. These memories will last a lifetime.

Each child will experience their own successes and their own failures. How they respond to that success or failure will go a long way to defining the kind of character they will exhibit later in life. I really believe that.

For the kid who handles the losses with dignity and the wins with grace, the foundation is set and the sky is the limit. For the kids that cry and fall to the ground kicking because they fail, their future can be as shaky as the foundation they are setting. In many cases, this is where it starts. Each young person can learn how to persevere and to overcome, to deal with adversity and conflict and to slowly learn to leverage each new challenge and experience into an understanding of who they are and begin molding who they will become. They don't know it at the time of course, but I believe it is important for us to understand this and help each child along on this critical journey for self.

So here we were in our first game of the Little League World Series regional qualifying tournament in Denver, Colorado. As the coach of this team, I sensed the nervousness and pressure that the kids felt in their quest for Little League immortality. If you win this tournament, you go to compete in the Colorado State tournament for a chance to play in the Western United States qualifying round in Waco, Texas. Beyond that lies the glory of a trip to Williamsport, Pennsylvania and an appearance on ESPN. This was the dream for all of the millions of kids out there who loved baseball and fantasized about making the Major Leagues. We were down by one run in the bottom of the 6th, (which was the last inning) with 2 outs and a runner on 2nd and 3rd base. My son Ethan, who was ten at the time, was up to bat. It had been a back and forth game and Ethan had pitched earlier and gave up the go ahead run. I could see it in his face that it was weighing heavy on him. With runners on second and third and two outs, he now had a chance to win the game with a base hit in what could be our final at bat.

I was so nervous and excited for Ethan that I thought I would burst out of my skin or just throw up right there in front of everyone. This was a big deal to him and admittedly, to me. Youth sports is not supposed to be about the parents but like most parents, save the crazy ones, I wanted Ethan to have a great experience and create a memory that would last him a lifetime. He was either about to be the hero or the goat on this day that much was certain. I could see the angst, fear and nervousness on his face and I thought to myself, this is what being a coach is about. This is what being a dad is about. I needed to be there for him somehow, some way. But I wasn't sure exactly what to do.

As I approached him in the on-deck circle and saw the big eyes of my scared little boy, I realized the moment that we were about to share was a moment that he would most likely remember for the rest of his life. I knew I would. I wanted to find the right words to say to him to let him know that no matter what happened I was still his Dad and that that would never change. I would always love him above anything else. Seeing the look in his eyes made me think of my Dad and the relationship I had with him. In that moment, I had a flashback to my Dad and one of the special moments we shared. I will never forget how he did that for me and how he told me everything I needed to hear without using any words at all.

*****

I was a high school senior and like most high school kids, I was completely lost. I had no idea who I was or what I was supposed to become. Up until that point in my life, all I knew about myself was that I was a football player. I was a good player, not great. What I didn't have in talent, size or speed, I made up for in heart and effort. It was 1985 and our team had just secured the AAA Pennsylvania State Championship football game at the Hershey stadium in Pennsylvania. As was customary, our coach called a timeout very late in the game. He did this to substitute players into the game so the seniors could come off the field and be recognized by the crowd, the families and all supporters of the program. This was a pretty big moment for any kid, but for a kid like me who knew it was the last time he would ever trot off a football field to a round of appreciative applause; it meant everything. I should have been basking in it but instead I felt a weight on me as if I would explode right there on the field. What am I if I am not a football player anymore? My eyes were filling with emotion as I hugged and high-fived my way through the sidelines filled with my team mates and friends. I could hear the crowd cheering for me and the other seniors. One of my best friends, Jay Wharton, was hugging me and whispering, "We did it! We did it! Never forget this day! I love you, man!" We were easily the two smallest kids on the team and we both knew this was it. It was over. We would never play again.

As I got to the bench, I saw my Dad down the sidelines. He looked at me with a satisfied, proud smile and he gave me the finger point. The finger point was such a classic thing that my Dad did. It was my Dad's signature way of telling me everything that never needed to be said. It meant that he loved me and that he was proud of me. It meant a lot to me right then to feel his approval and to know he was proud of me. I was not able to make it over to him yet, but I was glad. I didn't want to break down in front of everyone on the sidelines so I kept my distance.

Once the game ended there was a medal ceremony that lasted about ten minutes. It was a fitting end to a lifetime of effort and dedication to be crowned a state Champion, there was a wave of emotions building inside of me. This was the last time I would ever be wearing a uniform and playing football. I couldn't believe it. I knew that I had to go find out who I was and that everything I thought of myself was ending right there on that field. What was special about me without football? Who was I now? Who was I to become? In that moment it seemed to me that my entire life up until that point was culminating on that football field.

After the handshakes and hugs at the end of the medal ceremony, I remember finding myself standing all alone on the field. As the crowd began to disperse and the well-wishers parted, the world seemed to settle into a slow motion crawl. I was standing all alone and looking around me in this surreal moment in my life. The crowd up the field started moving and then parted. That's when I saw him, about thirty yards away from me. He was scanning the field looking for something. He was looking for me. It was Dad.

We began moving towards each other and I saw a look on his face that I will never forget. He seemed to know exactly why I was looking for him and just what I needed at that moment, he knew I was lost and scared. He was not always an over-emotional man. He was nurturing and kind and not afraid to say, "I love you," but he was strong and rarely did you see any cracks in the rock that was him. I don't even remember him crying at either his mom's or dad's funeral, I remember him being the strong one for his brothers and sisters. He was always the strong one.

I started moving towards him faster, feeling the emotion welling up inside me, ready to just let go. As I got closer to him I saw his chin tighten and his face contort as his eyes filled with pride, love and then tears. He hurried his pace to me. I put my head down and hurried to an equal pace as the emotion started pouring out of me. I reached him at the middle of the field and buried my face into his shoulder. Right there on the fifty yard line of Hershey stadium, I lost it and began sobbing.

"Hey, it's okay. It's okay. It's okay. I'm proud of you Peewee." I had that nickname from when I was a child because I was always the smallest in the class. It didn't matter now that I was 185 pounds and pretty solid. I was still Peewee to him. I could barely breathe. Then he said what I needed him to say. "I know" he said as he put his hand on the back of my neck in a strong embrace. "I know how you feel. It's not over. This is just the beginning for you, Pee Wee, trust me" he said as he smiled.

I gave him a strong nod of understanding and could only mutter out the words, "Thanks Dad" as I buried my face again. I never forgot that moment or those words. He knew just what I was feeling and he knew just what to say.

I desperately wanted to provide that same kind of

support and guidance to my own son now. I realized that this was one of those times with Ethan and I wanted to savor it.

Ethan stood in the on-deck circle, all fifty pounds of him and with wide eyes. He looked up at me as I approached him and he said, "What do you want me to do, Dad?"

The tying run was on third base, the winning run was on second base and there were two outs. The game was on the line, but it was more than that. This was my son, the first real, unconditional love of my life and I was torn between my competitive nature and my indefinable love and devotion to his perfect soul. I think most adults don't experience true unconditional love until they have their first child. That is when you really have that feeling that without a second thought, you would step in front of a moving train to protect them or to ensure that they would have a great life. At this moment I wanted Ethan to be okay more than anything and I wanted to help him however I could, unfortunately there were no trains around.

Without giving it too much thought I put my hands on his shoulders, looked into his eyes and as a complete calm came over me I smiled and said, "E, I want you to go up there, enjoy this moment, have fun and get a god-damned hit!"

The tension of the moment was lost in that comment and we laughed out loud. Seeing his reaction choked me up with a little emotion that was in danger of escaping me. Unbeknownst to him, I had a lump in my throat the size of Pittsburgh. He looked up at me laughing and turned to the home plate for to the first pivotal "at-bat" of his life. "OK, Dad!" he said with an air of relief and confidence that made me believe things would turn out well for him regardless of the outcome of the game. That moment between us had a clarity that no matter what happened, I loved him and he was my son. Just like my dad did for me. If he won, I would give him the familiar finger point that I always got from Dad. If Ethan didn't get a hit and the game was lost, I would be there to pick him up and tell him that I would always be proud of him no matter what.

This was a metaphor for the first major challenge he would come across in his life journey! This was going to be a part of the foundation of his character when times got tough! Whoa, that is a lot to put on an at bat in a little league baseball game.

My senses were alive as Ethan approached the plate. The atmosphere was electric and the crowd was in a frenzy. Ethan stepped into the batter's box, took his practice swings and waited for the pitch. He was facing Evan Garfield, an eleven year old man-child who was literally twice Ethan's weight and was topping fifty miles per hour on his fast ball. It looked like David vs. Goliath. Ethan left the bat on his shoulder and took the first pitch for a strike, the tension was mounting.

The crowd in the bleachers were hanging on to every pitch. The opposing crowd was encouraging their ace to strike Ethan out and win the game. Our crowd was shouting out encouragement to Ethan. He had a habit of looking at me standing outside the dugout in between each pitch. He would always look to me for support and encouragement.

On the second pitch, another fast ball, he hit a foul ball over the first base dugout. He was way behind the pitch. The count was 0 and 2 and things were becoming really tense, Ethan was down to his last strike.

He looked at me again and took a deep breath. I made a fist motion to him, which was a "You can do it. Stay strong," gesture. The pressure was at a fever pitch now and the crowd was going crazy. Hoping for this to be the last pitch of the game, they stood and cheered. Half of the crowd was cheering for Ethan to succeed. Half of the crowd was cheering for him to fail. Just like life. It seems like there are always people betting against you.

All we needed was a base hit to win the game. The pitcher threw the ball but Ethan didn't swing! The ball was just off the plate to the outside corner. Ball one. Ethan took the pitch at 0 and 2 in the biggest at-bat of his young life. It took real guts to take that pitch. I sure didn't want him to do that again. If he was going to go down, as in life, I wanted him to go down swinging. You can't get a hit if you don't swing. You can't get what you desire in life if you don't go after it.

*****

The parallels to the journey between a father and son through life were on display in this moment and not lost on me in the tension. He was standing tall and I couldn't have been more proud of him. The count was now 1 and 2. I clapped encouragement from the coach's box at third base as he looked at me again and I told him to "protect the plate" which meant swing at anything close to being a strike. I didn't want him to take another pitch. I loved that kid so much that I was trying to will him to do it. The fourth pitch came right down the middle of the plate!

Ethan made contact with it! He hit it hard on the ground heading for the area between the first and second baseman. It was a high chopper and had a chance to get through to the outfield. Since there were two outs, his teammates on second and third took off as soon as Ethan made contact with the ball. This was going to be close. Both kids would score easily if Ethan wasn't thrown out at first and I was already waving his teammate from second to go around third and head to home plate with the winning run. This was it.

The second basemen lunged to get the ball into his glove. It would have been an easy play to get Ethan out at first and end the game if he could catch it. Miraculously, the ball bounced over the glove of the second baseman and bounded into right field. The right fielder was playing in but he had no chance. He picked up the ball after Ethan's teammate rounded third and was halfway to home plate. He made a throw to home in vain that was halfway up the third base line as the teammate from second crossed home plate with the winning run. The crowd of parents, friends and supporters erupted.

Boulder wins! Boulder wins!

I looked across the infield and saw Ethan rounding first base; he smiled realizing that his hit won the game. He did it. He jumped up and down in excitement as all of the players, coaches and parents rushed on to the field to mob him and each other.

I just stood there, frozen, watching the celebration and started to cry. I couldn't hold back the rush of emotion that hit me. It was as if I had been blind my entire life and could suddenly see. I felt a warmth and peace that was pure, unconditional and eternal. I was so proud of him but most of all, I was so happy for him. This was an incredible moment

When the kids and parents were done celebrating, I approached him. The look on his face was an indescribable look of pure joy and pride with a hint of relief and gratitude. I picked him up in my arms and we hugged each other deep and strong as I whispered in his ear, "I love you, buddy."

"I love you too, dad." This was a moment we would remember for our entire lives.

One of his first real experiences with challenge and adversity was met with a will, determination and character that made me as proud as anyone could ever be. It is not an overstatement to say that it was one of the purest moments of love, pride and joy that I had experienced up to that point in my life. It made me realize that as much as a child has a complete surrender and a complete and total vulnerability to their parents, the vulnerability that a parent has to their children is equally as strong. You realize it the first time you hold that little infant in your arms and you realize it as you navigate every single day of their precious lives from that point forward. This was one of those memorable moments that make life worth living. We still keep a copy of the box score from the Boulder Daily Camera on Ethan's wall to this day.

After the glory and congratulations from the crowd died down, we headed to the car to go home. My phone buzzed, I looked down at the caller ID and felt an immediate dread.

"The show is over
Close the story book.
There will be no encore."

- Lyrics from Colorful, by The Verve Pipe

CHAPTER 2

I had always thought about what this moment would be like. I had been dreading it as much as anyone could and I always felt like it was just around the corner. I had been expecting it for most of my adult life and even in the last few years of my childhood. When I was four my Pop-Pop died (my dad's father) and I started to understand what death meant, I was terrified of my Dad dying. Seeing Pop-Pop laying in his coffin as a very young boy and watching the reaction of my family was startling and unnerving to say the least. Dad's family was not your run of the mill mourners. His brother and sister were throwing them-selves on the cascade, wailing and refusing to let go. It was traumatic for a little four year old kid. It scared me to death.

There is a certain indefinable, vulnerability that I had my whole life when it comes to my Dad and his health. Not that I wasn't afraid of my Mom dying too, I was. It was just different with my Dad. The bond most sons have with their father is unbreakable and my Dad and I were no different.

What would that dreaded call be about? Would he be dead? Would he be dying? What if he was all alone and scared? What if he was suffering? I used to wonder about that moment when you find out that your protector, your childhood hero, the rock of your life's foundation was gone. Or worse yet he was dying alone and afraid. What if he needed you and you couldn't get to him? That was my worst fear and one that I was about to face head on.

In a way, I would almost prefer that call to be simply

"He's gone." To see suffering, weakness and fear in him was worse than anything I could have imagined and more than I thought I could bear. I always wondered if I could find the strength in me to be what he needed in his final moments. Let's just say I had my doubts.

When I saw the caller ID, I just knew that Dad was either dead or dying. Somehow, I knew. I took the deepest of breaths, calming my racing heart and my sweating palms. I hit the answer button on my blackberry as my vision became cloudy through the sudden burning swell of what must have been tears. I had no idea the journey this call was about to set off.

"What's wrong?" I greeted my brother, Danny.

"Michael, Dad's down! He collapsed in Salzburg! He was standing in front of the Mozart museum and his heart failed. His heart stopped completely and he collapsed and split his head open on the street!"

I suddenly couldn't breathe. The world felt like it was closing in around me and like I was going to black out. "Oh, no!" were the only words I could manage.

*****

Later, I heard Dad's girlfriend and travel companion Marie relay the story of what had happened. Dad had been walking too much. He was getting tired and had to stop to take rests on several occasions. He was standing on the street in Salzburg; right out-side the door of the birthplace of Wolfgang Amadeus Mozart, which is a famous museum right in the heart of downtown. He loved Mozart. I can remember him playing Mozart endlessly along with other classical music. He loved it and as a result, I still have a soft spot for classical music. It makes me think of him.

Minutes after getting his picture taken in the doorway, he reached for Marie and said breathlessly, "I think I'm going to fall." Marie screamed "No you're not!" as she tried to grab him to hold him up, but she was not strong enough and down to the ground he went. His old, tired, half-mechanical heart was finally giving up. Dad had suffered heart disease for years. Of course, he always passed it off as Angina, but we all knew different. He also had 2 artificial heart valves. One was from a congenital defect from when he had rheumatic fever as a child and one was from having an old, weary ticker. All of the men in his family have suffered from something heart related, most ultimately dying from heart disease. So, I've got that going for me!

Danny continued, "The paramedics got to him within minutes and were able to resuscitate him. He is in the ICU on a respirator and for all I know he could be dying as we speak! Someone needs to go there and help him!" All I could picture was him lying face down on a cobblestone street somewhere in Salzburg, with his heart stopped, dying.

My brother Danny was talking fast but was in control as always. Danny was always in control in crisis situations. He was a state police officer in Central Pennsylvania and had seen his share of trauma and emergencies. He was in his element. My oldest brother, Rich, was quite the opposite. He was an emotional misfit and an alcoholic. And he was a mean one. He was the kind of guy that when he had too many to drink he would get angry and confrontational, ultimately wanting to fight.

When Rich would get blazed up he would often turn his attention and hostilities towards me, Danny was always the one to try and reason with him and for whatever reason, it worked. Rich and I were like oil and water ever since he went off to college. He was 4 years older than me, with Danny being the middle child. Rich would always look out for me when I was little and he may not have known it but I looked up to him quite a bit. I can remember being proud of who he was during high school but he changed in college.

Whenever someone would pick on me, especially Danny, Rich was there to give him a beating and to protect me. Then in college he began to expand his mind, and I am not talking about school. I saw him slipping away into something that troubled me; into something I didn't like. Into something I could no longer look up to; I thought he was a disgrace. I think the reason I am so mad at him to this day is I am just so let down and disappointed by him. We haven't spoken in years.

On the day of our mother's funeral, Rich decided to binge and drank all afternoon and into the night. Ethan and Christian were very young (four and two) and upstairs sleeping when Rich started blasting Mom's favorite songs on the stereo and weeping into his beer. This would have been a fine gesture with headphones on or in an empty house but Rich didn't really care that my children were sleeping and I was fiercely protective of them. I was determined that my kids were not going to experience such an unsettling site. There was a confrontation. There may have been a crime if Danny had not intervened. He took the sloppy, angry drunk asshole out back while Megan and I along with my two little children snuck out and went to a hotel at one o'clock in the morning. That was the last time I had spoken to my brother Rich in four years.

The oldest in the family was my sister, Janet, who was eight years older than me. She was very much a second Mother to me and my brothers but with a family of her own and a falling out of sorts with Mom and Dad, she was not around much anymore.

As I listened to Danny fill me in on the details, I felt panic rising inside me. Dad was slipping away and in real trouble. Apparently, the doctors were not able to communicate very well with us. They spoke almost no English and Marie was the only one we could count on to get semi-accurate information. As we discussed it and we realized how dire things sounded, we both knew someone was going to have to go.

I knew that trip was an awful mistake. I noticed his weakening state over the past year; I knew he was not up to a trip through Europe. For the life of me now, I don't know

29

why I hadn't stopped him.

"Is Marie with him?" I asked.

"Yeah she's there, but Michael, she's already talking about pulling the plug!"

A shudder swept through me and I froze as I immediately flashed back to when we pulled the plug on my Mom.

It was four years earlier and I was on one of many rotten business trips to Long Island, New York. At the time I worked for a broke, rinky-dink little start-up company that required five grown men to share a two bed-room apartment in a little town called Ronkonkoma. If it wasn't so ridiculously awful, it would have actually been comical. I used to sleep on a pull out futon in the corner of the living room while the CFO would chain smoke in one of the two bedrooms because his wife wouldn't let him smoke at home. The entire apartment would fill with smoke and he didn't give a damn. In the two years I worked for that company, I think that guy smoked a lifetime's worth of cigarettes. In the other bedroom, was the ultra-entitled son-in-law of the CEO who knew nothing about the business or our technology but somehow had gotten appointed as President of the company. It was nepotism run amuck. He would come and go at all hours of the night as if he was the only one in the apartment. I can remember him slamming the microwave each night late while I tried to sleep as he heated up fish sticks and ate Mayonnaise straight from the jar.

The other two poor bastards took turns on the different couches. It was miserable; I was miserable. It turns out that the CEO and the other founder were stealing from the company the entire time, even though the company was nowhere near profitability. They were living a lavish life in the Trump Towers in Manhattan and billing it all to the company. Thirty three hundred square feet on the sixty second floor with the best Manhattan view money could buy. Court side tickets to the Knicks, Center Ice for the Rangers. They even bought their own private island in the

Caribbean and built mansions on it. They were living the dream while I was sleeping on a broken futon and begging for fresh air. As things usually do, it all caught up with them. To avoid jail time, they had to pay the company back all they had embezzled.

One night when I was in my Ronkonkoma hell, my Dad called me and told me that Mom was in the hospital. He said she had a mild heart-attack and was in ICU under observation. She was seventy years old and seemed to be fading fast. She had also had a recent bout of bladder cancer and seemed much older than she actually was. I asked Dad how serious it was and if I should head straight down to Harrisburg that night. It was about a 5 hour drive. He told me that she was feeling better and that she was talking to my brother Rich before going to sleep. I was glad someone was there with her. I hadn't talked to her for about two weeks prior to this. It was too late for me to call the hospital and I didn't want to wake her up. For whatever reason, I decided to wait until the morning to see how she was doing; I would finish my meetings and then go see her on the weekend.

I wish I had gone when I had the chance.

When I got out of the shower the next morning at 6:45, I saw that Dad had called me. I didn't have a good feeling. I knew it was bad news, so I called him back right away.

It was the worst possible news. During the night, Mom had a massive heart attack and she was all but gone. They had resuscitated her but it was too late. She had lost too much oxygen to her brain, brain dead they called her. She was on a respirator but all brain activity had ceased.

Needless to say, I dropped everything and headed straight down to Harrisburg. It was a very long 5 hour drive. The longest drive of my life, to be sure. I can remember driving through a steady flow of tears as I beat myself up for not being there for her. I was the youngest in the family and she was always there for me no matter what. We had a special bond and as a child, I was the kid that would never leave her side. I was so attached to her, and now when she needed someone the most, when she needed me, I wasn't there.

I will never forget talking to Dad as I crossed the Verrazano Bridge from New York into New Jersey. I asked him to not pull any respirator plugs until I got there. He agreed. He also agreed to have a priest come and give her last rights at my insistence. I guess once a Catholic, always a Catholic. I also remember tears rolling down my cheeks while the radio played the song, "I'll be There for You" by Bon Jovi. That song always makes me think of that moment when I crossed into New Jersey as I rushed to be by her side, knowing that I was too late. It will always make me think of that moment and my Mom. The words were reflective of how she lived her life for me, my brothers and my sister until her final breaths.

I'll be there for you.
These five words I swear to you
When you breathe, I wanna be the air for you
I'll be there for you.
I live and I'd die for you
I'd steal the sun from the sky for you
Words can't say what love can do
I'll be there for you.

I don't remember too much else about that drive other than knowing I felt a pull. A sense of spiritual responsibility to get there, to be there for her as she took her last breaths. I had to let her know what she meant to me one last time. I hoped it mattered; I hoped it made a difference, I know it did to me.

As I arrived at the hospital in Harrisburg after what seemed like an eternity my brother Danny greeted me at the door. As usual, he was strong and in charge.

We spoke for a minute about the state she was in and how Dad was doing. We were both very sad but Danny was so strong. I had to be strong as well and hold it together. I was on a mission. I had to say my goodbyes before she was gone for good.

As I walked through the hospital hallways, my dread grew and grew. I didn't know what I would say when I got to her room. This was one of those moments in life that you just couldn't prepare for. I felt a panic rising in me again as I continued through the seemingly endless hallways. I didn't want any of this to be real and I didn't want to see her like this. I was also worried about my Dad; I had to help him through this.

I finally walked through the ICU doors and saw my Dad standing outside Mom's door. I immediately choked up. Dad looked so little, so fragile and so broken. I never realized how old he had gotten but it really hit me like a sledgehammer when I saw him. I couldn't necessarily remember seeing it in him until this moment. I had been so engrossed in my life, my kids, my marriage and my career that I had lost track of him, somewhere along the way.

I couldn't speak as he started to move towards me and held out his arms. When I got to him we bear hugged and I buried my face in his shoulder. In that moment at thirty five years of age, I was still a little boy hugging his dad for strength and comfort. He had tears streaming down his face and he kept whispering "We waited for you. We waited for you. Now you're here. We can let her go." I asked him if he was OK and if he needed anything. As usual, with a shrug of the shoulders, he dismissed the thought because it was never about him. He was a rock and was always the strong one. It took me a few minutes to gain my composure after seeing Dad and I asked if I could have a few minutes alone with Mom before so I could say my goodbye in private.

Dad gave me one more quick, strong hug and I went in

to see my Mom for the last time.

I knew it would be bad and I was prepared for that but I lost my breath when I saw her. She looked so old and tired, like she had been through hell; she was ready to let go. I immediately flashed back to a bowling alley in Harrisburg. I was little, probably three of four years old and sitting by her side while she played in her weekly league. I was the baby of the family, her baby, and I never left her side. I remember that occasionally she would put me in the day care room at the alley while she played, I didn't like it. I didn't want to leave her side and I put up a fight every time I had to. Now here I was as a grown man, rushing to get to her side one last time and kicking myself for being too late.

I thought back to our kitchen table where we spent endless summer nights sitting and talking about everything and nothing as the crickets chirped loudly. I remembered seeing the heat lightning in the distance as we talked and talked. It felt like magic to me, I always got goose bumps; I still do just thinking about it. It's funny what little memories stick with you. I remember how it smelled and how it felt when I would see the lightning bugs at dusk during the summer months. Every night the forest would light up with little flashes of light, like a million stars twinkling in the sky. It was a magical feeling, the kind that makes you think that maybe you aren't alone.

I thought about her taking my temperature by kissing my forehead when I was young and sick, or when she was tucking me in every night and kissing my forehead while she told me she loved me. She always used to say, "Goodnight. God Bless. I love you." I saw all of the moments when she nurtured me, gave me what I needed, and loved me without condition, with all of her heart and soul.

I pulled a chair up close to her because I was too choked up to talk. I held her cold, gray hand and bent down close to her ear. Her legs were a growing shade of purple as the blood was pooling inside her. Her heart could barely pump anymore, even with the machines she was attached to. Her hair was a mess, her face contorted and blocked by the breathing tube. I managed to swallow down my emotion and say the only thing that came to mind.

"Thanks Mom. Thank you for giving me a great life. I will always remember you. You will always be with me and I will always love you. I will always be that little boy who wouldn't leave your side. It's OK to let go now, OK? We are going to unplug this machine and let you go. It's OK for you to go now, OK? It's OK. We love you."

I kept hoping she would open her eyes, I was hoping for a miracle. I hoped for her to acknowledge me with her soul and tell me she was going to be OK. I hoped to feel something. One last bit of magic. I silently prayed for one last lightning bug in the trees.

But there was nothing. She didn't say a word. She didn't move. There was only the rhythmic movement and sounds of the respirator. She was gone; to my eternal failure and shame, I was too late.

My last words to her, if she could even hear me, were words that came naturally to me. The final words I ever spoke to my Mom were "Goodnight. God Bless. I love you" just like she had done to me as a child all those years ago. I choked on the last part as I kissed her on the forehead.

Danny had come in the room and put his hand on my shoulder, my brother Rich, to my astonishment was not there. He was sitting at home watching golf on television and drinking beer. I guess everyone handles crisis situations in different ways

My sister Janet had a major falling out with my mom years before and was not there. I always hoped Janet didn't have feelings of regret for not being there.

Dad came in the room with the doctor and the priest. Then the doctor said a few words that I completely tuned out. And then he turned the machine off.

And that was that. There were no trumpets. There were no angels. There was no music. There was nothing. There was complete silence except for the occasional sniffle or choking back of tears.

The priest said one last prayer, blessed Mom and anointed her forehead with holy oil as he said the ashes to ashes line and something about commending her spirit back to God. It was so surreal that I was frozen and not able to speak. I couldn't take my eyes off of her. I watched every last breath as they became slower and slower. Her lips were starting to turn purple. The breaths were now coming more infrequent and in short, labored heaves. Her bottom lip gently trembling as the last bits of air seeped out of her lungs. I couldn't help but think about the fact that she was there for my first breath. She nurtured me through every breath from then until now and here I was standing beside her as she drew her last. I had wished for something more, some kind of spiritual awakening or connection but there was nothing. It was the emptiest, loneliest feeling I can ever remember.

Dad came over and bent down, picked up her hand and said his thanks to her for their life together, the good and the bad, kissed her on the lips and walked out of the room, shaken but strong and dignified. I had to look away because I was starting to lose it.

Finally, silently and peacefully, after about ten minutes she stopped breathing altogether. I was there for every single last one.

As I watched her now lifeless body, my mind swirled back to happier times. I could picture her smiling on Christmas Eve and on one of our birthdays. I could see her laughing with her sisters and the neighbors. There is one picture of her that I still have, from the 70's. This is the one I choose to think of when I think of her. It was Christmas time. Christmas time was always the favorite time of year for everyone in our family. Mom included. The family was always at peace on Christmas. It was a time of great love, thankfulness and togetherness. It was a picture from when we were the kind of family that makes you remember the good times. The picture was her with her red, poofy nineteen seventy's hair. She was wearing a white sleeveless sweater and was proudly presenting a plate of cheese, crackers and shrimp to the camera. She looked so happy. That is why I remembered it. She was so happy that day. Life was not always happy and not always perfect, but when I think of my Mom now, this is the time I choose to remember. It was the best of times for our family.

There are really no words that can explain the feeling of watching your Mom take her last breath. I was feeling a mix of deep sorrow and guilt, but I also felt gratitude. I was thankful I could be there and to see her at peace and to let her go.

I was aware she was dead but I couldn't stop thinking about how cold she might be. I became irrational and asked the nurses to keep bringing heated blankets for her. The nurses were very sweet and accommodating and though I could barely get out the words to say "Thank You" to them, we appreciated it. When I left her hospital room she had five heated blankets on top of her.

"Is it at that point already?" I asked Danny as I started choking up a little, remembering those final moments with Mom.

"Marie is in a hotel in Salzburg and she said that she can't stay much longer".

"Has anyone spoken to the doctors"?

"I have only spoken to Marie and she said that the doctors don't speak English".

"OK. Well, we need to talk to the doctors before anyone thinks about pulling any plugs, agreed? "

He agreed.

"Marie has said that she can only stay a few days longer. The trip wouldn't give them a refund and she can't afford to stay in Salzburg. It's too expensive."

"Tell her we will pay for her lodging. She can't leave him alone there! "

"I already told her that. She is scared and upset as you might imagine."

"Look. I understand that but she needs to be there for Dad until one of us can get there."

"Michael. She is an old lady who is scared and alone in a foreign country. One of us needs to be there for Dad. One of us should go. "

"There was a pause of silence. We both knew who he meant. "

"Can you do it?" He asked.

"Of course, I'll go. Let me look into flights and I will get back to you. How do you want to involve Janet and Rich?"

"Let's call them and talk through it. "

"All right, we can use my conferencing service. I will email everyone the number. Let's dial in 30 minutes. "

Danny agreed to call Rich and Janet and tell them.

"OK, talk to you then", I said.

CHAPTER 3

The last time I talked to Dad before "the call", I was wishing him farewell on his whirlwind European vacation with his new girlfriend Marie. Ever since Mom died 4 years earlier, Dad had been very lonely. I tried to check in with him as often as I could, but with my demanding job, 2 little boys and my marriage on the verge of collapse, I was only able to get in touch with him once every ten days or so. I was so happy to see that he found someone to spend his time with. I regret that I was not able to see him or talk to him more often but my own life was a bit of a train wreck in the making and it was easy to lose sight of what was most important.

Dad was always happy to receive my calls. When we spoke, it was like old friends getting together over a beer. The talks were never long but we seemed to be able to say what was needed. He never really understood what I did for a living so we didn't talk about my work very much. We didn't need to. He was proud of me and I always knew it just like I knew the sun was going to come up every day. We would talk about the usual; his work, how he was feeling, the kids, the weather, his dog, and the Steelers. We would always talk about the Pittsburgh Steelers. No matter what time of year it was and no matter what was going on in our lives at the time.

When you are a kid growing up in Central Pennsylvania in the 1970s, Pittsburgh Steelers football is a way of life. It is a religion and a bond shared between fathers; entire families and communities. We were no different. Every Sunday at Dad's house when the Steelers were playing was like a holiday. Some of my fondest childhood memories revolve around Steelers football and my Dad. Whether it was a crisp fall day, a rainy November afternoon or a snowy December morning, it felt like football and most importantly it felt like home.

Each year when the weather turned, Dad would start a fire early in the day and keep it going well into the night. We had an old brick fireplace that stretched the entire length of the back wall in our family room in our old house in Harrisburg, Pennsylvania. It felt like we were camping out every time he would start a fire. He would sit in the back by the fire with the logs crackling and the smoke floating up the chimney while he smoked his pipe and drank his beer. The dog would lie at his feet while the rest of us gathered around the TV. I remember how he would sit on the edge of his seat like he was just taking it all in and he didn't want it to end. Those days are still so vivid in my mind. It was always a special time.

When we got home from church on Sunday mornings we would rush out back and scavenge the woods behind Dad's house. We would look for kindling wood, twigs and sticks; anything that would help start the fire. We'd gather old newspapers, magazines and catalogs that we had been saving all year just to get the blaze going. I remember the smells of the first sparks of the fire and now whenever I happen to smell a wood fire, I think back to those magical days in Harrisburg and I think about my Dad.

When I was little, I would bring my toys downstairs and play with them on the floor while we readied for kickoff. Mom would be making her special spicy tomato juice on the stove and it filled the house with the sweet smell of tomatoes, Tabasco and spices. It was perfect, everyone was happy.

Then the world would stop for 3 hours and we would cheer for our team. We would debate play calling, yell at the TV, high five each other and ultimately revel in victory or lament the rare defeats. We shared and celebrated week after week and year after year. I will never forget those days and I will always love the Pittsburgh Steelers. It's about so much more than a football game or a football team. It's about a time and a place and a series of special moments between us and our Dad that no one can ever touch or take away. It's about being together with the ones you love.

When Dad and I talked down through the years, we would delve into every aspect of the Steelers and their teams. We would debate personnel decisions, the draft, the rivalries with the hated Raiders and Cowboys in the 70's, and we would fondly remember the glory years. We would talk about everything. Pittsburgh Steelers football, above all else, no matter what was going on around us, was a calming elixir we would literally share together until his last days.

The one thing that always stuck with me and made me feel for him after Mom died was how lonely he seemed. He hated to eat alone, it always depressed him. In spite of everything Mom and Dad had been through in their forty years together, he missed her and it broke my heart to see that. I asked him to call me whenever he sat down to eat alone, but he never did. I would gladly talk to him while he ate, but that wasn't his style. He was as low maintenance as anyone ever has been or will be. He used to make us laugh every year when we would call him on his birthday. He would sigh, take a deep breath and say in as under-stated and sincere way as possible, "It's just another day."

Dad was a strong, unassuming, self-effacing man dedicated to his family and his profession. He was a family doctor for more than forty four years and in spite of his years of success, he had a streak of insecurity that was brought on by decades of an at times loveless and at times abusive marriage. Like any marriage, Mom and Dad had their good times and their bad times.

Mom was an angry drunk and Dad was a classic enabler and threw back too many himself. Over the years, Mom grew to resent Dad for the success he had in his career. The crazy thing is, I realized that my own marriage was heading in the same direction. Megan was becoming more and more resentful and focused on "everything she gave up for me", rather than feeling fortunate to be together and for what we had. By the time Mom died, Dad had no ego left and rarely shared his days with anyone. I was beginning to know all too well how he felt. It's not that they didn't ultimately find peace and companionship with each other, but when I think about their life I feel very sad because there was a lot of real pain, heartache and shame. I guess every family has their secrets and their dysfunction. We certainly had our share.

Through it all there was the kind of indefinable loyalty and love for each other, where you would have jumped in front of that same train that I was searching for on the baseball field. It was a different era. They were at times awful to each other but if someone outside the family would cross any one of us we circled the wagons and fought for each other. It wasn't perfect back then but we just knew we had each other's backs. It doesn't always feel that way anymore. It certainly didn't feel that way in my own marriage and it was about to get absurdly worse than I could have ever imagined.

It is heartbreaking to me that Dad felt like he could never share his triumphs with anyone; least of all his own family. That must have made him so lonely for so many years. I wish I had been old enough to understand it and to do something about it for him. I was very cognizant of it now and went out of my way to take an interest in his work. I prodded him for details and stories from his years as a doctor and as the fine man that he was. I tried to be a good son to him because I could see he needed it.

There is an interesting dynamic we all experience from childhood to our final stages of life. It starts with our parents are our heroes and role models, then in our middle years we push them away as we seek to establish our own independence and identity. In the grandparent stage, we face what it's like to be a parent on our own and we reach new appreciation for our own parents. But nothing prepares you for the final stages of their lives when we have to be the strong, parental ones and ultimately have to watch them die and bury them. To see weakness, frailty and fear in their final moments creates a kind of a hollowing out of the soul and a loss of the ideas we formed about who our parents were. It can be a lonely cavern of emotion and pain and I was about to learn just how lonely it could be.

CHAPTER 4

Dad's new girlfriend Marie was a bit of a whipper snapper with a sharp wit and a tendency to needle him. She drove me nuts, but Dad loved her. He loved the attention. He loved the fact that someone cared and that she was genuinely impressed by his career. The first time I met her and we went out to dinner, I was taken aback at the playful banter between them. Dad was positively glowing. I wanted to toss my cookies but I can honestly say that I can't remember seeing him smile and carry on the way he did, ever. Part of me was so happy for him but part of me was devastated too. Here he was at seventy six years old nearing the end of his life, and he was finally able to be himself. He was actually flirting. He was finally able to love his life and be embraced for who and what he was.

Dad was not exactly a world traveler. He spent time in Germany while he was in the military but he had been deeply rooted in Pennsylvania for 50 years. He never ventured any further than South Carolina for the occasional family trip to Myrtle Beach. Heck, he wouldn't even leave Harrisburg when Three Mile Island was about to melt down in the 1970s. I remember being in 5th grade and being evacuated from school, I was scared. I wanted to run as far away from Harrisburg as possible, but not Dad. He never even started the car. He had a patient who worked at the plant who assured him that everything would be fine, and that it wasn't close to being a meltdown like the news was reporting. We were the only ones in our neighborhood still at home. Dad was grilling hamburgers out in the driveway drinking a beer without a care in the world. I am glad his faith in his nuclear engineer patient was rewarded and that disaster was averted.

Somehow, Marie convinced Dad to take a European vacation to Germany, Austria and a cruise on the Danube to Budapest and Hungary. It was hard not to notice in recent years that Dad got tired easily and couldn't walk very far due to his accelerated heart condition. I didn't think the trip was a good idea at all, but I said nothing. I didn't want to judge or meddle in his relationship. I figured Dad was not the kind of man who would agree to such a trip if he didn't really want to go, and he sure as hell didn't allow anyone to tell him what to do; including me. So I said, "Good for you! Have a blast." I figured they would take a lot of taxis and tour buses.

CHAPTER 5

I don't know how I ever let myself get to the point where I felt so lost and devoid of answers in my life. I can't pinpoint any specific time or event that got me to this place. It was more of an accumulation of things over time. Things such as, living month to month and questioning the faith I was brought up to believe, to struggling with my own questions of spirituality and religion and waking up one day and realizing you are married to the wrong person. The weight of it all stifles your ability to be who you are or to be the best you can be. Couple all of that with daily responsibilities of taking care of kids and things can start to clutter your mind and distract you from real happiness and a real existence. This is definitely where I found myself.

Now that Dad was at the end of his life, my questions about my own life, the afterlife, God, and all of the stories I was taught to believe, were colliding with my struggle. What a comfort it would be to think that as Dad "passed over" someone would be there waiting for him and help to make his transition to the afterlife loving and peaceful. If only I could believe it. If only it was real.

Over the years I had slowly and painfully arrived at the position that there was nothing beyond death, despite my sincere desire for the opposite to be true. For most of my life I have gone back and forth between believing it and believing it was all just people needing hope that there was something glorious awaiting us beyond the pain and suffering in our lives.

After Mom died, I was certain I would be able to feel her or connect with her spirit in some way. I wanted to see one more lightning bug in the trees, just like I prayed for while she took her last breaths. I was always in search of some kind of proof, some-thing tangible that I could see. Something I could hear and feel in order to prove that there is more to being than the life we make here. I went to see a medium after Mom died but I quickly learned (after the Archangel Gabriel visited me, or so the kook said, because I was special), that it was all bullshit. I was so desperate to feel her and to know it was all real, that I tried several alternate forms of spiritual searches.

In all of my expeditions for spirituality, I never felt a thing that was real. I would love to believe that some people have a special talent to see dead people and bring their message from the great beyond, but I can tell you that I didn't find any of them. My experiences had soured me completely on the possibility of communicating with people that have passed.

However, there was this one time where I had the most vivid dream. I can't remember when, but I remember going to bed one night asking my Mom to come to me or give me some kind of sign; a way to communicate. I woke up in the middle of the night. My heart was racing, I was emotional and a feeling of elation swept over me. It was like I had just seen a ghost. I had the most vivid dream and it felt so real that I wasn't sure it was just a dream or maybe something more.

In my dream, there were faceless movers in glowing white outfits that had just finished moving Mom into her "temporary apartment." That is what she called it. She was talking to me; she was so peaceful, happy, young and beautiful. She was explaining to me that this was where she was to stay until we were ready to cross over; this is where she would wait for us. She couldn't contain her happiness. There was a brilliant light shining around her. She was holding our little dog, Max. He was a white haired toy poodle and he was always my Mom's favorite. She was holding him just like she used to when I was a kid. Even dream Max was happy and friendly, which was something I wasn't used to. He used to bite me all the time when I was a kid.

The whole time I was struck by how she seemed. She was clearly still my Mom but she was also clearly different. She had a sense of "knowing" around her. That is the best way I can describe it. She knew all of the secrets that she couldn't tell me about life and death. She knew that she was waiting for us. She knew it was only a temporary place for her. She knew we would all be together soon. She knew so much more than she could tell me. I didn't want to leave, it was the most peaceful feeling I had since she died.

I woke up after the dream in the middle of the night and I am not ashamed to say that I started to cry. It was so real and so profound that I wanted to go back to sleep and visit her again, to learn how she was and what it was like on the other side. Unfortunately, I never felt her beyond that night.

I think a lot of my doubts and uncertainty has to do with questions about faith that I have been struggling with all my life. It is very easy to evaluate my religious upbringing and the stories I was taught as exaggerations or misinterpretations. God knows there's enough skepticism in the world. I guess over time, I became skeptical too.

Religion was a big part of my life all the way up through high school. Going to a private Catholic school from first through twelfth grade certainly contributed to that. There was religion class every year. To their credit, the Catholic schools I attended were open to teaching about other religions and philosophies alongside Catholicism so that we could compare. I can say that even at forty years of age, I am thankful for the religious education I received through the Catholic programs I grew up in. I am more knowledgeable about religion, the Bible and Christianity than most people. It also gave me a well-rounded perspective on religion vs. spirituality that had a large role in shaping what I believe and how I have been able to classify myself as "spiritual but not religious."

"Spiritual but not religious" is really just another way of saying, "I really don't know. I want to believe in something, but I have no idea what it is or how to connect to it." I have spent most of my life hopeful that there is something out there, but I just don't know and I don't have the faith or conviction to say for sure without seeing for myself.

Mom and dad were devoutly religious when I was growing up. We would participate in all of the Catholic customs, from first communion through confirmation and all of the church's holy days of obligation. We went to Sunday mass every week.

At home, there were crucifixes in each room of the house with a printed message on them that said, "Peace to all who enter here." There was also a picture of Jesus in the hallway at the top of the steps which was accompanied by an incense urn. Occasionally, I would see Dad stopping there and praying, usually when the family was going through tough times. I did all the stuff I was required and expected of me. I attended the masses, said all of the prayers, and sang the songs. I performed all of the required sacraments and I believed everything that I was taught to believe; but I never felt it.

I never really connected to anything associated with religion and I never really understood it. I would listen but I never really heard. It was never real to me; it was just something I did because I was supposed to. Once I was old enough to have the choice to participate in religion, like many others I chose not to. As I grew older I began to drift further and further away from all of it.

My compass was definitely off due to years of unhappiness in a faltering marriage. Being with the wrong person can affect you so much that if you stay in it long enough, you wake up one day and look in the mirror unable recognize yourself. I remember thinking to myself, "how did this happen?" I truly believe that as an adult, one of the saddest moments that anyone can experience in their lives is the moment you realize that your marriage is over. It involves a combination of emotions ranging from failure to fear, uncertainty to dread, anger and finally, a fatal surrender. A surrender that says no matter how bad my life gets, no matter how hard this is on my kids, it's better than being in this relationship.

It took a lot for me to get there. I was programmed to suffer through it and let the emotions fester until periodic arguments over the years exploded and built on each other as we moved further and further apart. After 14 years of it I knew our marriage was over and that we didn't love each other. It wasn't worth it to us anymore. It wasn't worth it to me anymore. She didn't love me and I didn't love her.

The decline of our marriage started out slow. There were little things along the way. A little comment here or there, a little less touching or loving each other over the months and years. Then the distance keeps expanding. You find yourself avoiding the conflict or the coldness, working more and doing anything you can to not face the emptiness and its implications. At some point, things fall off a cliff and you find all kinds of reasons to spend time away from each other. By ten years into the marriage, Megan didn't even come to the door when I got home from work. There were never any hugs waiting, let alone any higher forms of intimacy. Before you realize it, you have become roommates and not necessarily even friends.

Megan had developed a pretty strong resentment towards me. First was my work, then my sense of humor and eventually my entire person. She always saw things as though I put everything ahead of her. Our whole lonely existence together was a struggle for my time and my attention. Whatever I did was never enough to fill the emptiness she felt. The fear of splitting up paralyzed me and led to inaction. I vacillated between numbness and general acceptance of the misery of my life. This position leads to intense introspection causing you to question why you are putting up with something so much less than happiness in the short lifetime we all have. It is easy to get into a rut but sometimes it seems impossible to climb out.

I knew the time had come for tough decisions but I was scared. I was terrified and I knew she was too. We had vowed to take care of each other. We promised each other that we wouldn't be like other angry, bitter divorced couples. Once I got Danny's call, Megan became very supportive, caring and focused on taking care of the kids while I took care of Dad. I figured we could deal with things when I got back.

CHAPTER 6

This conference call would be the first time I've spoken to my brother Rich since my Mom's funeral. It would be awkward but Dad's needs were most important here.

We all got on the line and he said, "Hey little brother."

I said, "Hey." And that was pretty much it.

Talk about anticlimactic. The least he could have done was offer an apology! "I'm sorry I am a drunk asshole" would have sufficed but all I got was "Hey little brother." He wanted to talk to me about as much as I wanted to talk to him, so we moved on quickly.

Danny had gotten an update from Marie in time for our call. It was good news, considering the initial reports we had gotten. Dad was off the ventilator and breathing on his own. Rich had called right away and was able to talk to him. He said he didn't sound so good, and that he sounded a little crazy. He could hear him yelling "get me the hell out of here!" at the doctors when they spoke. That part made my heart sink and I felt for Marie being there alone, it must have been pretty overwhelming for her.

They say doctors make the worst patients and that was definitely true in Dad's case. It made me cringe to think about him screaming and being scared, not understanding what was going on around him. He sounded very disoriented. It made me worry that he had suffered some brain damage due to lack of oxygen before they resuscitated him.

Through Marie, the doctors had said he was stable for now and that he needed 21 stitches on his forehead. Ouch. It was hard to imagine what he might be going through.

We talked about "what if" scenarios. What if he didn't improve? What if he died without one of us there? The thought was hard for all of us to take.

My biggest and most immediate concern was when did Marie have to leave? I didn't want Dad to be over there alone. We knew that she was going to have to leave in a few days; she had said that she didn't have enough money to stay much longer. We told her that we would reimburse her expenses, but we realized that she was in an awful position and we couldn't expect her to extend her stay. Her vacation was ruined, her companion's heart failed and she was all alone in a foreign country she had never been in before. It was a lot to ask.

It was clear to everyone that one of us needed to get to Salzburg as soon as possible to relieve Marie. We needed to be there for Dad, and for whatever was going to happen next. In the back of my head, I already knew how this was going to end up.

As we discussed who could go, the excuses came one after another.

"I have to work."

"I don't have a passport."

"I can't leave my dog."

And then, finally, "I can't afford it."

"Michael, you are the only one who can afford to go to Europe at the drop of a hat. Can you do it?" my brother Danny asked.

I didn't hesitate. "I'll go," I said. I didn't look forward to this kind of trip and being in Austria for God knows how long, but I relished the opportunity to be there for Dad. I had no idea how I was going to handle work but I knew I could figure it out and my employer was incredibly understanding and accommodating when it came to family. I would adjust my hours and still be able to stay on top of things at work while helping Dad at the same time. I had already planned it in my mind that I could stay with him during the days and then once he goes to sleep, I could go back to my hotel and work late into the night.

The truth is I wanted to be the one to be there for him. I may have been the baby of the family, but I could see now that I was the one they all needed to count on. And as much as I dreaded what was ahead of me, I wanted to be there for Dad.

"Thanks, Michael."

"Yeah, thanks little brother."

I thought to myself, "I am doing this for Dad. I just hope he can stick it out until I get there."

The only problem I had was finding a day to go. I felt I needed to wait for a week due to some pressing issues at work. As if all of that wasn't enough, my company was planning to close an office and lay people off in Pueblo, Colorado. As the VP I was expected to go and announce the changes. I was also responsible for notifying the people who were to be let go. The layoffs were scheduled for Monday and it was now Wednesday. I needed five more days. I needed Marie to stay with dad until I could get there, but I wasn't sure she was going to. As long as Dad was still in stable condition, I thought I had some time. Against my better judgment, I decided to wait, just like I had done with my Mom. I hoped it turned out better this time.

CHAPTER 7

I hung up the phone and sat on the back porch in a rare moment of quiet reflection. My mind drifted and I began to imagine how scared Dad must be to be in a foreign country, near death and unable to communicate with those around him. I just kept saying to myself; hold on Dad, I'm coming. I will get to you; I just need a few days.

Different moments with my Dad from my childhood started coming back to me in the quiet. Through it all, Dad was the anchor. Some moments were more poignant and memorable than others. Some were more forgettable and regrettable. Some were embarrassing, and one was downright devastating.

My mind settled on one particular, unforgettable and awful moment where Dad was not only there for me but one where he literally saved my life. It is not a moment I ever talk about much. In fact, I don't think Megan had ever really heard the whole story.

It happened in 1973 when I was five years old but I still remember it like it happened this morning. Now that Dad was lying in a hospital bed on the other side of the world, I remembered how he saved me and I hoped I could save him, thirty five years later.

It was mid-December and I was getting myself primed up for Christmas. Christmas meant everything to me and I would spend months leading up to Christmas Eve trying to decide what I was going to ask for from Santa Claus. The

Sears catalog that came every year was well worn out by the time December rolled around. Mom and Dad made the magic of Christmas come alive for me and my siblings every Christmas. It was always the best time of the year.

No matter what was going on in our family or in our lives, everything stopped around Christmas time and we had peace and togetherness. They were special times.

As a child, I loved how it smelled at Christmas time. There was a distinctive smell of cinnamon, pine and garland from the wreaths that was mixed in with the seafood from our annual Christmas Eve feasts.

I always loved the crisp air after a real snow on a cold day. It left the landscape enveloped in white and a perfect eerie silence all around. Cars moving in slow motion in almost shrouded silence. The entire world slowed down and felt renewed. I can still picture all of the branches draped with a new fallen powdered snow, it was magical.

Rich, Danny and I would play football in the snow in the front yard while my Mom hung our wreaths and put garland around our lamppost.

I loved the carolers and the tinsel. I loved how everyone was nice to each other; I couldn't get enough of it. I loved the excitement of waiting to open presents and anticipating what each box had inside of it.

I loved seeing my brothers and sisters open presents and I loved when my Mom and Dad loved each other.

It was all perfect.

Mom was great about putting out extravagant Christmas decorations each year. She had made the ceramic Santa's and Frosty the Snowman decorations herself. They meant the world to me. When she would unpack them, I was almost beside myself knowing that it was almost Christmas.

She also made a white ceramic miniature Christmas tree. It had a light bulb inside it and glass colored tips on each of its branches and miniature snowflakes all over it. I loved looking at it, especially when the lights were out, and it glowed in the dark. I had it shipped to me after Mom died but unfortunately it was destroyed in shipping and arrived in about fifty seven pieces. I was devastated. Years later when my son Christian was three years old, he was invited to a birthday party at an arts and crafts workshop. I took him to the party and found a very similar white ceramic Christmas tree with colored lights and snatched it up. I never even looked at the price. I still don't know how much I paid for it; I just signed the credit card receipt. That tree has a permanent and special place in my house each year for the holiday season because it reminds me of my Mom and of special Christmases in my family.

Above all else at this time of year, I loved the lights. Colored, blinking Christmas lights were my favorite. I wanted them around me all of the time. After our Christmas Eve feast we would head out to decide the Peterson neighborhood Christmas decoration awards. We used to walk around the neighborhood just to see how each house was decorated. We would pretend we were the judges of the neighborhood contest and pick a winner each year. It was always a fun time.

I loved that we always bought a real Christmas tree, going shopping for it was always an adventure. We would each lobby for our favorite tree and Dad would be the ultimate decision maker, breaking the inevitable ties each year. The night we brought the tree home was always one of the best nights of the year.

Once the tree was standing, the fun really began. We got to string the lights on the tree. Nat King Cole, Andy Williams and the Harry Simeone Orchestra would blare in the background as we wrapped the lights around the tree by the fireplace. We ate chocolate chip cookies and drank soda while we sang along with each carol unabashedly.

Some years it would take hours and even days to get all of the lights working.

One cold wintry day around lunchtime in December

1973, I was sitting in the big bay window in our kitchen waiting for my Dad to come home for lunch. I used to sit there looking out to the street until I could see his car. Then as he pulled into the driveway, I would run outside and jump into his arms, screaming "Dad!" It must have been a great daily welcome for him.

I sat down and had lunch with Mom and Dad. I had my usual, a peanut butter and jelly sandwich and a bowl of Campbell's Chicken Noodle Soup. It was my favorite.

As I finished my lunch, Mom and Dad were still talking and eating, I decided to head downstairs to play with my toy T-Rex and my six million dollar man action figure. I had an active imagination and was planning an elaborate and epic battle between Steve Austin and the man eating Rex. As I got downstairs, I noticed that the Christmas tree lights were off. That wasn't going to do.

At five years old, I didn't understand electricity but I was pretty sure I knew how to turn the Christmas lights on. I went over to the other side of the room and flipped the light switch up to the on position but nothing happened. I looked around for another light switch. I saw one on the other side of the room and went over to try that one. Nothing.

Then I saw a brown extension cord on the brown carpet leading to the white outlet cover over top of the brown paneling. You get the picture. It was your typical "down and brown" seventy's house with brown everywhere and bright orange curtains and a plaid orange couch. It was hilarious. The Brady Bunch had nothing on us.

I noticed that the cord was not plugged in so I walked over to the wall, picked up the plug and plugged it in. Still the Christmas tree did not light up. I followed the cord from the outlet to the other end and then I realized that the lights from the tree were not plugged into the extension cord.

I was determined and was not going to accept defeat; I was going to see those colored lights blinking. I grabbed the Christmas lights cord and the extension cord and tried to push them together. The lights flickered on for a second but did not stay on.

I looked down and noticed that the cord was only half plugged in, exposing the metal prongs of the Christmas tree cord. Somehow I had plugged the fat male prong into the skinny female receptacle on the extension cord and now it was stuck. I knew something wasn't right and tried to pull the lights apart from the extension cord, but it was in there pretty tight and I couldn't pull it out. I tried again. Still nothing, and no lights on the tree. I tried two or three more times but no luck.

Then I got an idea. Instead of calling Mom or Dad and asking them for help, I thought if I could put one end of the cord in my teeth, I could yank the other side out more easily. So I tried it.

As I put the cord into the right side of my mouth and started to pull, the corner of my mouth slipped around the protective coating on the extension cord and made contact with the half exposed metal prong, instantly sending a flow of 110 volts of electrical current through my body.

My body froze in intense pain and excruciating heat built up on my mouth as the voltage coursed through me. I was paralyzed. I couldn't move and I couldn't pull the cord from my mouth. I couldn't see anything. My vision was black and white snow, like when your old cable TV would go out. All I could hear was an intense buzzing sound and all I could feel was the pain and heat growing worse and worse. It was unlike anything I had ever felt until or since that moment.

Electricity and the human body are not compatible. The electricity will burn the skin around its entry point significantly, reaching temperatures of more than 200 degrees. It was literally beginning to char the flesh around my mouth, but that wasn't the critical and most dangerous part. Right now, the electricity was traveling straight to my heart and beginning to cause ventricular tachycardia, or for lack of a better term, it was killing me. I only had a precious few seconds left before it might be too late and the damage would be irreparable and fatal.

A lot of what happened next, I do not remember for obvious reasons but I was told later about my Dad's heroics that day.

Mom and Dad heard the intense buzzing sound downstairs and knew something was terribly wrong right away. As they reached the top of the stairs of the split level house, their eyes filled with horror as my Mom screamed hysterically, "Michael, Oh my God, NO!!!" Dad was screaming my name, "Michael! Michael!" I can't imagine what that scene looked like to them. Seeing me paralyzed and convulsing as the electrical current flowed through my body, bringing me closer to death with every second.

I was in serious trouble and wouldn't last much longer. Until the day she died, Mom would never talk to me about it. I think she blocked it out of her mind, all she would ever say was it was the worst day of her life and she just wanted to forget about it.

There was no time to lose. Dad hurdled down the 7 or 8 steps in one jump and bounded over Steve Austin and Rex to get to me. I was an electrical conduit at that point and if he had touched me then he would be electrocuted as well. He knew that of course and so in one swift move, he jumped to my side and with his rubber soled shoe, kicked the cord that I was holding and broke the hold I had on it, flinging it out of my mouth and harmlessly to the floor.

As the cord fell to the floor, so did I but as always Dad was there. He caught me before I hit the floor. With urgency in his voice he said, "No. No Michael. No. No!"

Technically, I was dead. The electricity had stopped my heart and burned my face terribly. Dad laid me down on the floor and started resuscitating my limp body and screaming for Mom to get him some ice and to call 911 for an ambulance. It must have been a parent's worst nightmare coming true.

In very little time, he was able to get my heart started

again and had applied a bag of ice to the side of my charred and swollen face. Mom was hysterical, screaming and wondering what was happening to her youngest son. I was in shock and barely alive. How much electricity had gone to my brain? Was my heart damaged? Would I ever see or walk again? Would my face be disfigured if I survived? These were all valid concerns.

The ambulance arrived; Dad was holding me in a blanket and holding the ice bag to the side of my face, silently strong as his shoulders shuddered just the slightest bit. Mom was on her knees by my side crying my name and praying to God for me to be OK.

The paramedics arrived and Dad gently laid me on the stretcher as Mom wept uncontrollably. Dad held the ice on my face and stayed with me in the ambulance, all the way to the hospital. I don't remember any of it. I don't remember any white light or spirits or anything while my heart was stopped. All I remember before that is the pain. But for some reason, maybe fate, or maybe luck, I survived.

Over the course of the next several years, I had multiple surgeries to repair my face via skin grafts and other early plastic surgery repair techniques (which were not so commonplace in the nineteen seventies). I am left with a permanent reminder every day when I see my face in the mirror. Looking back now, I don't think about the pain or the horror of that day as much anymore. Instead I think about what my Mom and Dad must have suffered through and I think about how lucky I was that Dad was there that day. If he wasn't home and if he wasn't a doctor and a hero, I surely would have died on that December afternoon in 1973. He saved me that day and I now hoped to have the chance to save him by bringing comfort to his final days.

CHAPTER 8

The next three days went by without much incident, which was a relief to everyone. Dad seemed to be getting a little stronger which made me think that maybe I wouldn't have to go at all or at least we could delay it so I could take care of my work commitments. In fact, things were looking so positive that they were planning to move him out of the ICU and into a private room the next day. At the time, I thought to myself that Dad was like Rasputin. Nothing could kill the guy! He had been through two bypass operations, two heart valve replacements and had been life-flighted on a helicopter to Temple University hospital in Philadelphia after his second open heart surgery (because he was not recovering and was in congestive heart failure). He survived all of that and for a moment it seemed like this old, half mechanical tough guy might be able to pull out of this as well.

As things were steadily improving, Dad was able to talk to us a few times over the phone. The first time I got to speak to him was heartbreaking, he was nuts. He slurred his words and told me that they were doing experiments on him and that I needed to get there right away to get him "the hell out of there." I had a knot in my stomach and it was one of the worst moments I can remember. It hurt to see him losing his mind like that.

I still wondered if he had suffered brain damage due to the lack of oxygen or maybe it was the medication that they had him on.

I convinced myself that it was just the medication and that he would be better once they moved him to a private room.

So the next morning I procrastinated at the office, waiting until he got to his private room before I called him. When I finally dialed and was connected to his room, he answered and my fear faded away as soon as I heard him speak. It was Dad; he was back again and sounded very much like his normal self. We had a conversation about how much he was looking forward to getting home. I didn't ask him much about what the doctors were saying. He couldn't shed much light on it at that point. The fact that he was already talking about coming home told me all I needed to know. He was the strongest man I had ever known and he was down but not out. I told myself that in a month, we would be sitting in his living room watching the Steelers and drinking a beer together.

When I spoke to Marie, she told me that they said he was improving but that he was still very weak and could suffer a relapse at any moment. She was asking me to come in the next day or two because she had booked her return trip for the next day. She didn't want to leave Dad there alone, but she could not stay.

The doctors were not committing to him being discharged anytime soon so Dad would be alone for a few days. It seemed OK to me because he was getting stronger and sounding more and more like himself every day. Marie even said he had a little bit of an appetite, which is always a good thing.

With Dad showing improvement, I was thinking about pushing my trip back. I hadn't bought the tickets yet and decided I could take my time and focus on my work for a few days. I knew I didn't want to leave Dad alone over there for very long but I still had critical things I needed to take care of. Something was gnawing away at me in the back of my mind. I was doing the same thing I did when my Mom passed. I was making something else more important than rushing to get to my Dad. I continued to press the thought down and decided he would be fine for a few more days.

As I sat at my desk looking out over the Rocky Mountains and thinking about how strong my Dad was, my mind shifted to a vivid childhood memory where I could have sworn he was a super hero.

It was an unforgettable day back when I must have been no more than a 2nd grader, so I was seven or eight. It was at a football game. There were lots of football games between me, Rich, Danny and Janet, who was a cheerleader. This time it was my brother, Danny's game.

I remember the day quite clearly, as I don't think you ever forget the first time you see someone die right in front of you.

It was a cold, gray and a rainy early afternoon in November. The sky was overcast and there was an eerie darkness over the town and the field. It was almost foreboding, as if something was about to happen. I was sitting on the top row of bleachers next to my mom, watching our Holy Family Jets battle the Good Shepherd Deacons.

There was a fence separating the bleachers from the field. Dad was on the sidelines coaching my brother's team, he was the team doctor for all of our teams from first grade through high school. Sitting on the end of the bench from Mom was Sean Burrows' dad, Roger Burrows. Sean was on the team, playing on the line with my brother. Roger was probably in his early fifties or maybe his later forties. He was not a healthy looking person. He was quite overweight and more than a little sloppy. His face was gray and he had unwashed, oily hair. He was not overly friendly and seemed a little off. Dumpy was maybe the best way to describe him.

It was starting to mist a little and dense fog was settling in overhead. The surrounding trees gave the field a feel of an old forest with fog covering their tops. It was a great setting for a football game!

There were maybe three or four spaces between Mom and Mr. Burrows. It was well into the first quarter when I was compelled to look over in Mr. Burrows' direction. His face was turning the strangest color of greenish-purple that you can imagine. I may have only been seven years old but something didn't seem right. I was scared and I knew that something was seriously wrong. I whispered to my Mom to look over at Mr. Burrows and as we turned toward him, he had become really purple-green now. He had white bubbly foam coming out of his mouth and he was slumping, when he suddenly collapsed over the side of the bleachers. He fell from the seventh bleacher row down to the frozen ground below, face first in a messy heap with a thwap and a weird, awful gurgling sound.

Everyone on the bleachers turned toward the noise and there was an "Oh my God!" and general hysteria broke out. People were really freaking out and I was growing more scared. Some were running over to try to assist, some were just looking and gawking, some were crying and some just had their hand over their mouth in horror.

In every crisis situation, there are gawkers, criers, paralyzed onlookers and finally, there is usually a hero. Amidst the chaos and commotion, my Mom managed a shaky shout towards the field. "Mike! Mike!" she was able to cry out. She did a great job because I saw my Dad turn to the sound of her voice and when he saw her face he knew something was gravely wrong. She pointed to the area where Burrows had done his face dive and as soon as Dad figured out what was happening, he leaped into action. Literally, in two swift motions he stepped to and hurtled himself over the fence, landing feet first on our side. He then deftly ran through the crowd to get to Burrows. "I'm a doctor, let me through!" he exclaimed as he rushed to his side. The crowd parted like the red sea. In nineteen seventy five CPR was not as commonplace as it is today.

Dad flipped Burrows over onto his back, put his arms at his side and raised his head from the back of the neck. He then raised both of his arms over his head with his hands together in a fist and proceeded to lower a devastating karate chop right into Burrows' chest. Whoa! I later learned that that little karate-chop actually broke 3 of Burrows' ribs.

Dad began performing CPR and doing chest compressions. I kind of knew what he was doing because I'd remembered seeing Hawkeye Pierce do that on MASH. There was a crowd around Dad and Burrows now and the ambulance and paramedics arrived just a few minutes later. Dad fell back off of Burrows, exhausted, as the paramedics took over. The color had returned to Burrows' face which I took to mean he was going to be OK. Dad had been able to resuscitate Burrows' heart and save his life.

I remember watching him fall back off of Burrows, as if in slow motion. To me it was like Superman flying off over the horizon after he stops the train from derailing, saving hundreds of lives of innocent women and children. In Dad's case, it may not have been hundreds of innocent women and children, it had only been ole sloppy Burrows, but it didn't make a difference to me. He was still my hero on that day.

CHAPTER 9

Just when things seemed like Dad was out of the woods, the unthinkable happened. Marie had been gone for just over a day when my brother Rich called and got the awful news that his heart had failed once again. He had been trying to stand up in his room and collapsed to the floor, smashing his head open for the second time.

They were able to resuscitate him and move him immediately back into the coronary care unit. Things were falling apart. He had now survived dying twice. We all started wondering aloud how much longer this could go on and if he should be resuscitated if it happened again. We were quick to agree that we wanted him to be kept alive unless one of us was there to be with him the next time he crashed.

The awkwardly translated message that came next from the doctors was clear. If anyone from the family was going to come, they needed to come now. His heart was extremely weak and damaged; he may not make it through the night.

I was heartsick that I hadn't gone when I'd had the chance. Now I feared that it was too late. It was the same thing with my Mom all over again. I immediately began trying to find flights.

My best option was a Lufthansa flight from Denver to Munich, Germany with 1 day notice. The price was almost six thousand dollars for a round trip open ended ticket. Once again, everyone agreed that I should be the one to go and so I booked it. I put the cost of my ticket on my American Express card and decided to worry about it later.

Having lived in Switzerland for a period of time in the nineties, I had been to Southern Germany several times and had also been to Salzburg. I would figure out the rest of the trip later but for now, I was relieved I was able to get a seat on a flight leaving at noon the next day. I was going to be on that flight no matter what.

Then I realized that I was one day away from my commitment to shut down the office in Pueblo. How was I going to do this? I needed to be at the Denver airport boarding my flight at the very time we were scheduled to notify the employees that their jobs were being eliminated. I called my boss Stan and told him about my situation. He was tremendously supportive and agreed to go in my place. I told him I would be on the phone to talk with the team in Pueblo, It was the best I could do given the situation.

My head was spinning. There were a hundred little details that I knew I was forgetting. I figured that I would work them out once I got there. There were train schedules to learn, money to exchange, I had to get my phone enabled for international calling, and I had to find a place to stay. I also had to think about what Dad might need and what I needed for work. The list was endless.

As I was going over a list in my head, it hit me that I didn't even know the name of the hospital where Dad was. I had my brother Danny call Marie to get me the name before I left. Dad was in a place called the Universidad Krakenhouse de Salzburg. I assumed that it was the only hospital in Salzburg and that it would be easy to find once I got there. Beyond that, I didn't give it any thought at all.

I packed a backpack with a few days of clothes, my laptop and some work related items. I couldn't believe I was heading back to Europe again, and under the worst possible circumstances. All I could think of was how I hoped he made it through the next day so I could get to him. I hoped and prayed that I was not too late like I was for my Mom.

It was late now. Megan had given the boys their bath and got them ready for bed. I tucked them in and read them stories. I told them that I was going on a long trip and would be gone for a little while. They took it in stride, but they were a little too young to really know what was going on. It was much harder for me to say goodnight to them, not knowing how long I would be gone for or when I would see them again. After getting them to bed, I took a long shower and got into my own. I started thinking about Dad and what he was going through. He had been alone now for three days. None of us had been able to talk to him since he collapsed for the second time. He must be in bad shape, I thought.

Sleep was not coming easy to me. My mind once again, began drifting off. This time, I was remembering the first time I was taken away to the operating room for surgery on my face after my accident.

I was five years old and my face was scarred and charred from the electricity. I needed a skin graft to replace the damaged skin and for other general repairs thankfully, that was the only lingering effect from all of the voltage that coursed through me. Mom and Dad were in my hospital room with me at six thirty in the morning when there was a soft knock on the door. They were here to get me and take me to the operating room.

I was so scared. I didn't want to go. I didn't want anyone touching my mouth and hurting it more. I quickly ran over to my Dad and asked him to pick me up; I was crying now and begging him.

He knew I was scared but he also knew I had to go. He promised to stay with me the whole time and that he wouldn't let anyone hurt me. I was squeezing my arms around his neck as hard as I could and I was determined to not let go.

Unfortunately, the nurses who came to get me were stronger than I was and they were able to get me on the gurney and strap my arms and legs down. I was terrified and screaming now at my Dad "please, please doesn't make me go!"

Then I saw one of the nurses take out a needle and test it to make sure the medicine was in it. I started squirming and screaming to let me up and begging them to not put that needle in my leg.

My dad asked them to stop for a minute. He leaned down close to me on the gurney and spoke soft and comforting as he looked into my eyes and promised me that he wasn't going to let anything happen to me and reminded me that he would be there the whole time. He was able to distract and reassure me as they quietly and quickly gave me the shot. They then wheeled me down the hallway and into the elevator. He never left my side. He held my hand the whole way.

We got off the elevator and went through another seemingly endless hallway. We got to the doors of our final destination; Dad wasn't able to go the rest of the way with me. Whatever they had given me in that shot was making me sleepy and I didn't have the urge or the strength to fight it anymore. I looked over at Dad as he was letting go of my hand. I still remember the look on his face. He looked so sad and as if he was sorry that I got hurt and that I was having to go through this. As they wheeled me away, he promised me one last time that he would be right there when I was done. He would be there waiting for me.

Once in the operating room, I was strapped down to a new table. There was an intensely bright light above me shining on my face. It was so bright I couldn't open my eyes. I don't remember anything else. But I remember his promise to be there for me.

After the operation I started coming out of the anesthesia, he was there just like he said he would be. He talked me through it, told me not to be scared and that he would never let anything bad happen to me.

As I lay there, the same damning thoughts kept cycling in my mind. Oh God! I should have gone when I had the chance. What if he dies alone? Why was I so selfish?

I don't think I slept for more than 20 minutes that entire night. I needed to get to Salzburg as fast as possible.

CHAPTER 10

My day started at 6 AM on Tuesday. Although I hadn't gotten any sleep, I was running on adrenalin which kept me wide awake. I decided to get out of bed and be productive, seeing as I did not know how long I would be gone or what would be waiting for me when I got there. I was hoping for the best but expecting the worst. I just kept hoping that he could hold on until I got there. I also hoped for a smooth flight so I would be able to sleep on the way but I am a poor sleeper on airplanes so wasn't counting on it.

I spent the morning on work phone calls, getting everything in order for the layoffs, and organizing my calendar. I tied up all of the loose ends that I could, because I was expecting to be "disconnected" for a day or two. I was on the phone for most of the drive to the airport. I was discussing the logistics of the layoffs and the communication plan. They were setting up a speaker phone for me in the company meeting area so I could hear and say a few words. It would be awkward as hell but under the circumstances, it was the best we could do.

I was able to reserve a window seat near the back of the plane. It wasn't ideal but it was all they had. It was a ten hour flight which would be brutal, but with a window seat, maybe I would get some sleep. I remained hopeful.

The check in at the agent desk started out fairly routine and uneventful. The agent was a nice lady in her early 50's. Her name was Samantha, Sam for short. She was very pleasant. When she asked me if I had any bags to check and I said that all I had was my backpack. She then asked me if I was heading to Germany on vacation. "No ma'am. I am urgently trying to get to Salzburg. My dad was there on vacation, his heart failed and he collapsed. They were able to bring him back twice but they said he may not survive the night. I am rushing to get there so he doesn't die alone."

I choked a little on that last part. I must have been wearing it on my face.

"Oh I am so sorry. You poor thing." There were two agents now, they stepped back from the desk with my passport and began talking and clicking at another computer.

"Can I see your boarding pass hon?" Sam asked.

She took my boarding pass and tore it up, printed off a new one and handed it to me.

"We all wish you the best of luck to get there for your Dad, and I hope he makes it. We are upgrading you to first class. You can also go sit in the Lufthansa first class lounge until the flight is ready to leave. Please enjoy your flight and God Bless You and your Dad, OK hon?"

I was so stressed out and caught off guard by her act of kindness that I had trouble getting out the words to thank her. My eyes filled up as she looked at me with compassion and knowing. I whispered "thank you very much" and She nodded a "your welcome" as I walked away.

The seat that they just gave me was $8,000 on the Lufthansa web site the day before.

I made my way up to the Lufthansa club lounge, got a glass of orange juice and found a quiet cubicle. I sat there looking at my surroundings and thinking about how surreal this all was. It was already time to connect to the conference call. I was not looking forward to this. I really just wanted to get going as fast as possible, but I also realized that these were people's lives as well and I didn't take that lightly.

The call started with my boss Stan announcing that the reason we brought everyone together was to notify them that we were going to be shutting their office down as a part of a restructuring. Most of them would be affected immediately. He explained that the company had prepared generous severance packages and outplacement services to help them land on their feet. The reality was that in their remote town in Colorado there were no other high tech jobs like this available. In all likelihood, they were going to have to settle for menial jobs that paid half of what they were making otherwise they would have to move. Moving was not an option for most of the people there who swore to spend the rest of their lives in the beautiful, secluded place.

I could hear a little chatter in the background but it was mostly stunned silence.

Just then, as Stan asked me to say a few words, I heard an announcement to start the boarding of my flight. I was going to have to be brief. I spoke from the heart.

"I want to thank you all for the contributions you have made to me and to the company over the years. I apologize that I can't be there with you in person today but I want you to know that I am very proud of the work we have done together and that having the ability to represent all of you was an honor and a privilege."

I was interrupted by one of the employees saying that they all understood my reasons for not being there, and that they were praying for my Dad. I guess word spread quickly.

"Thank you very much for that. I appreciate it more than you know." I was touched by such compassion for me and Dad while they were facing a life changing announcement. I will never forget that.

With that, I wished them all well and thanked them for time. I promised to help them transition in any way I could.

I hung up and took a deep breath, grabbed my backpack and headed to the airplane. I was feeling guilt for what I had just done and for having left Dad laying their alone. I was stressed to the max.

As I hurried through the terminal, my mind drifted to another source of guilt that I carried. Dad's retirement party was after Mom had died and was sprung on him at the last minute. I was very upset that no one in the family knew about it. No one was there for him and the healthcare company Dad was working for did a horrible job "celebrating" the end of his 44 year career as a doctor.

Dad wasn't fired or laid off but he was "encouraged" to take his retirement. He was seventy four years old at the time, and the business side of medicine had weighed him down to the point where it got in the way too much for him to love it like he used to. I remember him saying that he would miss his patients dearly but that he wouldn't miss the "assholes that ran the place." That was classic Dad.

I didn't even find out about the retirement party until a few weeks after it happened.

I was traveling for work to the east coast and decided to travel through Harrisburg and spend a night with Dad. I knew he always appreciated it when I did that so I did as often as I could. I noticed some greeting cards on the table and a few pictures of Dad at his party. He was having a plaque and a cake presented to him. I asked him what it was for and he told me about the party. I could tell he was feeling a little embarrassed about the inauspicious way they celebrated his career and because none of our family was there. I was immediately pissed.

I asked him why in the world he didn't let me know about the party and that I would have gladly come earlier to be there. Janet and Rich and Danny would have been there for him as well. His answer was predictable. A little shrug of the shoulders and a "you guys are too busy". That was so like him, he never wanted anyone to make a fuss over him or to be inconvenienced.

He handed me one of the cards on the table, he was getting quite choked up as he said "this is what it's all about.

This is why I did it for all those years. Not for their stupid plaque!"

The card was from a woman whose daughter had cancer at a very young age. Dad treated her and made the initial diagnosis, got them to the right oncologist and consulted on her treatment. In the letter, she was thankful and poignant as I read it. I saw Dad watching me and I could feel his pride and emotions swelling.

"Dear Dr. Peterson.

We heard you were retiring and I had to send you a note to let you know what you mean to me and my family. When Lizzie was initially diagnosed, you were great. You were compassionate, straightforward and when things got the hardest, you were always there with a strong shoulder for us to lean on, we will never forget you for it.

Now that Lizzie is in remission, we thank God for her health and we thank God that we had you as our Doctor for all of those years.

You will be missed but never forgotten.

Thank you so much and God Bless you for all you do!"

I looked up at him as he wiped the tears from his eyes. I was really happy for him and I was really proud.

I gave him a big hug and said, "This is the best retirement gift I can think of. It sure beats the hell out of that stupid plaque. Let's go get a beer!" We both laughed, he put the card back on his table in its place of honor.

We went to dinner together and had a beer. I asked him stories about his years as a doctor. I could tell he was happy to have someone to talk to about it. He shared many great stories that night.

One of his stories was when he sold Mom's car after she died. There was a young woman who worked at his office for many years in a support capacity as a receptionist and records keeper. She was raising her children alone and was struggling to make ends meet. Dad had said he always noticed how she drove a "beat up" old car and how she would sometimes be late when she was having car trouble. He noticed her one day getting out of a cab in front of the office. When he asked her about it, he learned that her car had broken down again and the cost of the repairs was far beyond what she could pay. She seemed desperate and scared. Dad sold her Mom's car, a Honda Accord with less than ten thousand miles on it for one dollar. She was overcome at the gesture and offered to pay him more; in fact she offered to pay him all that she could scrape together (which was around fifteen hundred dollars). Dad wouldn't have it. He said he wanted to help her and didn't need anything else back from her. He deflected all other comments or praise about his generosity. No one even knew what he had done. That was so him.

I was happy to be there for him that night and hear his stories and I was proud to be his son. It was a good night. It was also the last night I spent with him before the trip.

CHAPTER 11

I quickly got settled into my $8,000 first class seat and had a glass of wine in my hands in no time. This seat had everything you could ask for. My own private media center, a reclining bed, comfortable blankets, pillows and all the booze I could drink.

The flight was scheduled for almost ten hours and was set to land at 6:30 am the next morning. I was very thankful for the agents who were kind enough to allow me such comfort for the trip to Munich.

As the plane took off I realized that in my haste to leave and complete the conference calls I forgot two things. One, I hadn't had my company set me up for international dialing so my phone was not going to work when I arrived. I decided I could figure that out when I got there. Two, I didn't even know if Dad was still alive. I didn't have a chance to check in with anyone before the flight took off. It was very unnerving and all I could think about were the doctor's words; "he may not make it through the night." At this point, I could only sit back, try to relax and hope. My plan was to have a few drinks, eat dinner and try to get some sleep. I knew it was going to be a long, rough day when I got there.

At about two hours into the flight, I had finished a surprisingly wonderful meal of Cornish hen, stuffing, potatoes, salad, bread and a bottomless glass of wine. Gourmet cooking at thirty-five thousand feet was pretty incredible. I was very grateful. I was also feeling the wine. I thought I could get used to living like this.

I decided to turn everything off, recline and try to get some sleep.

Sleep was not going to come easy though and in the end it did not come at all. I laid there for an hour with thoughts of Dad, hoping he was doing OK and praying that I wasn't too late. Memories started flooding my mind.

As a kid, the phone would ring at all hours of the night because Dad was on call. He always took the calls and he never complained. I used to listen to some of his calls and was struck by how calm and comforting he seemed. I always wondered who was on the other end of the phone and what they were going through. Every once in a while when there was an emergency, he would tell them to call an ambulance or go to the hospital immediately and he would have to go. I would wait up for him for hours until he got back to see if the patient survived.

I remembered sitting on the back porch with him listening to the Philadelphia Phillies baseball games while our dog chased birds, rabbits and anything else that would enter his domain.

I remembered Dad at Christmas time. Christmas was always our favorite time of year. He was known to have a few beers and sing Nat King Cole's Christmas album at the top of his lungs. Some years, we all would join in.

Every Christmas Eve was the same. After the sun would set, we would all gather by the tree with the fireplace popping and cracking. The dog was always afraid of the noise from the fire and would sit up at the top of the stairs and watch the goings on from a safe distance.

Dad would turn the music off and remind us all of the true meaning of Christmas. Every year, he would read the gospel of Luke from the Bible, the story of the birth of Jesus. And every year, he would choke up when he read the part about the angel saying, "Fear not, for behold I bring you good tidings of great joy which shall be for all the people. Glory to God in the highest, and on earth peace, good will toward men.

He would take a second to collect himself and then he would say, "Merry Christmas. I love you all." We would all hug and wish each other a Merry Christmas.

The music was put back on at full blast and Dad would proceed to hand out the presents one by one. Once they were all distributed, we would dig in and take turns. We savored the night and opened our presents as a family.

He always hid one present for my mom and pretended it got lost before magically finding it behind the couch cushions, or tucked under the tree. One year he got her a diamond ring that made her cry. It was a very nice moment and we all got a little choked up seeing their love for each other.

We would have our annual Christmas feast. Steamed shrimp with Old bay seasoning and flounder stuffed with crab meat. It was always the best meal of the year and the best night of the year.

Once I realized that I wasn't going to sleep, I decided to sit up and open my laptop. I opened up Microsoft Word, created a new document and started writing. I was writing things about my Dad and his life that I didn't want to forget. As the memories came to my mind, I wrote them down so I could share them later.

I didn't realize it at the time, but what I was writing was the beginnings of his eulogy. The words flowed easily. I recorded everything I knew about his childhood and his life. I wrote about the kind of man, friend and father he was.

I literally wrote for all but two hours of the flight. When I looked out the window in a rare moment of distraction from my writing, I noticed the sun was breaking across the horizon below and that Europe was just starting to wake up. It was the fastest ten hours of my life.

With only about an hour of the flight left, I saved the file, closed my laptop and went to the washroom to clean up.

As I settled back into my seat, I started planning my first moves I would take when we got to the Munich airport. For some reason, I could not remember the train system in Germany and I was planning to catch a train directly from the airport to Salzburg. You know what they say about the best laid plans.

CHAPTER 12

As the plane touched down in Munich, I felt a little surge of energy. I was now approaching two days without anything more than a few restless hours of sleep.

It felt surreal to be here in Germany again. I hadn't been to Europe in over ten years. I knew I wasn't here to relax or do any sight-seeing. I was on a mission to get to Dad but I hadn't really considered anything beyond that. There was plenty of time for that in the days to come. At least, I hoped there would be.

I still didn't know if he was alive and my anxiety level was growing with every step. As I walked briskly towards the connecting train station outside of the airport terminal, I decided to check for a signal on my cell phone to see if by some miracle I could make a call. I wanted to call the hospital to find out if Dad was still alive and how he was doing. I turned on the phone, and as I expected, I got no service. I decided that I would wait until I got to the train station and then I would find a place to call. In reality, I was scared to know the answer to the question.

When I got there, it took me several minutes to realize that this was not the main train station in Munich. In fact, the Munich airport was forty kilometers away from the Munich city center and is only served by the local and regional trains.

There were no trains to Austria from this station, much to my despair. Further research made it clear that I needed to take a train from the airport to the Munich station and from there I could take a train to Salzburg. I was deflated when I learned that it was going to take me at least another hour to get to Munich. There were two options for the train and they ran every 10 minutes.

I did the only thing I could do. I bought a ticket to Munich city center and got a Coke and a sandwich and headed toward the train. The sandwiches in Germany were very simple but very tasty. I got a ham sandwich with cheese and butter on the bread, just like I used to get all those years ago. They also make great individual serving pizzas. I bought one of those for the ride to Salzburg and got on the train.

I had to hurry to get to the next train so I decided I could call to check on Dad's status when I got to the main station in Munich. I unknowingly chose the regional train that made multiple stops in the surrounding areas around Munich.

By the third stop I realized I had gotten on the wrong train and that it would take an hour and a half to get to downtown Munich. A little planning might have gone a long way here. Immediately, my mind wandered to Dad and whether or not he was OK. I was hoping and praying that he was still alive. Any delay in getting there was excruciating for me. He needed to hold on for a few more hours.

The seats on the regional train were very old and stiff, like an old bus and they were not very comfortable at all. The train was packed with commuters starting their day. They got on and off the train in droves at every stop. Some on their way to somewhere. Some on their way from somewhere. It was all one big blur to me in my desperate and sleep deprived state. I started getting very frustrated and began counting the minutes left to get to Munich. My anxiety continued to grow to a fevered pitch. I needed to get to Dad as fast as possible.

After the first 20 minutes I started losing consciousness and dozing off in between stops. There wasn't much scenery to note on this route, so my mind wandered to better, simpler and happier times.

I could picture Dad in the summer, outside manning the charcoal grill with a beer in hand. He would be cooking hamburgers or his favorite, a London Broil steak. I could smell the meat cooking and imagine what it would taste like. I would love to have him cook for everyone again. As I drifted in and out, I was comforted by these thoughts and was transported back home.

After what seemed like forever, we were finally pulling into the Munich station. I was feeling exhausted but motivated to quickly find the first direct train to Salzburg.

As the train slowed to a stop, I stepped out and headed straight for the main ticket window. It was easy to find as most of the signs had some English or were easy enough to understand. I found a window with a short line and waited impatiently. My fear was that a train was going to leave any minute and I couldn't afford to waste another two to three hours. Finally, there was a break in the line next to me and I went for it.

"Sprechen Sie English, Bitte?"

"Yes, how can I help you," came the first friendly reply since I landed in Munich.

"I need a ticket to Salzburg, Austria please on the next train out!" I hurriedly said. By this time, it was now almost ten in the morning. This trip seemed like it would go on forever. Still, my thoughts were of Dad and getting to him before it was too late. "Please God. Help me get there to him in time." I silently prayed.

"Yes, of course." She said as she typed furiously at her keyboard.

"There is a train leaving in 15 minutes". The cost is one hundred and forty euros, which was about one hundred dollars at the time. I paid with my credit card so I could hold on to my cash in case I needed it. I got my ticket with very little time to spare. I checked my blackberry once more, but there was still no signal. I could see many people getting on the train. I had to get to it and find a seat as we were within 10 minutes of leaving. I decided that there was not enough time to find a payphone and make a call. I would fly blind until I got to Salzburg. I still didn't want to know. I had been traveling now for more than sixteen hours and hadn't slept in more than two nights and I was feeling it. I hurried to the platform, made my way through the crowd and hopped onto the back of the train.

It was late July and the temperature was rising steadily without a cloud in the sky. It looked to be a brutally hot day. As I checked my watch, I figured I could get to him by one o'clock. I shuddered to think what I would be walking into when I got there.

CHAPTER 13

The train was absolutely packed. I passed through at least 5 cars without finding a single open seat. It was getting hotter by the minute and I was really tired so I decided to try my luck and head into the restricted cars to find a seat. This was the equivalent of business class seats on an airplane.

These were the cars that had individual compartments that could seat up to 6. After seeing that the first 5 or 6 were full, I found one with only one person in it and I asked if the seat by the window was taken. The answer was no so I quickly moved to it, put my bulging backpack on the luggage rack over my head and sat down. I now had sweat rolling down my back and my forehead and was beading. Unfortunately, the window seat I chose, was directly facing the unfettered sun, baking me even more. The heat was becoming oppressive and I was pretty uncomfortable. I pulled the sun shade halfway down the window and got my sandwich out while I waited for the train to leave.

The train started creeping slowly out of the station right on time.

Finally, after sixteen and a half hours, I was setting out on my last leg of the journey. I pushed the thought that I might be too late out of my mind and settled in to enjoy the countryside.

Over the next two and a half hours of travel through the German country-side, the Bavarian and Austrian Alps, I bobbed in and out of a restless sleep. I could never sleep comfortably sitting up and the heat was stifling as the sun continued to beat down on me. The car had filled up, with every seat taken, which made it even harder to sleep. I dozed in and out of consciousness, and was jostled awake with every major bump on the tracks. The sun seemed to beat down on me no matter where the train turned, even through the shade screen.

As I drifted, I pictured his dead body lying there when I arrived. My worst fear was that he waited for me and I didn't go when I had the chance. Just like my Mom. These haunting images would pop into my head and then I would suddenly wake up.

I was really in need of some restful sleep. I wished I could lie down but the only place to lie down on this entire train was on top of it!

After two and a half hours the train started making a few stops on the outskirts of the city, I could tell we were getting close to Salzburg. I was almost there, my anxiety continued to grow.

After what seemed like the longest journey of my life, the train slowly pulled into the main station. It felt like I was entering a different world in a different time.

Salzburg is a truly marvelous, cultural wonder. It has picturesque mountains, beautiful Baroque and Medieval architecture with lakes and mountain streams galore. It is an amazing place to visit and soak in all that it has to offer. But all of that was lost on me at the moment.

My heart beat with anxiety and expectation and more than a little dread. I waited all of this time to find out if he was still alive. I was here now, but I was scared to find out. I just kept thinking, "what if I didn't leave in time and he died scared and alone?" The hospital couldn't be that far. I was just going to find my way there instead of wasting precious minutes making phone calls that could literally mean his life or death. I was close. I was so close. I hoped I wasn't too late.

CHAPTER 14

As the train crawled into Salzburg ever so slowly, I readied myself to rush out of the station and to the hospital. I left the compartment which had become a sweat box, and headed to the nearest exit so that I could leap from it as soon as the train stopped. It was very hot and humid and my shirt was sticking to me. The fact that I had no idea where the hospital was seemed only a minor nuisance to me at the time. I figured it would be easy to find an English speaker who could tell me how to get there. After having lived in Switzerland for two years, I was not worried about being able to communicate. I was now approaching twenty hours of travel time and my third day without any meaningful, restful sleep. I could feel my fatigue growing but all I could think about was getting to Dad in time and the panic and dread I felt about being too late.

I convinced myself that he was still alive because I would have felt something if he had died during the night. Marie had left five days ago and Dad had been all alone this entire time. When the train finally stopped, I leapt off and began weaving my way through the crowd, through the shopping and ticketing areas and straight out the main entrance. There were taxis parked and ready. "Thank God! I'm almost there, Dad! I'm almost there!"

I decided to fire up my blackberry again to see if by some miracle my international dialing had been enabled . Still no luck. "Fuck it", I thought, "I will be there in ten minutes," I reasoned and decided to not check it again.

I hustled up to the first taxi. "Sprechen Sie English, bitte?"

His reply was simple and uninterested. "No." Oh boy, I thought.

"Taxi to Hospital Universidad Salzburg, bitte?" I tried anyway.

He shook his head no as if he didn't understand me or wasn't interested in taking me anywhere. I found it a little odd but given the hurry I was in, I decided to move on to the second taxi.

After a similarly frustrating experience with the second taxi driver who also didn't speak English, I decided to move on to the third one. I had made my mind up that it was the last one and then I would try something else.

When the third taxi driver did not speak English and was not able to understand where I was trying to go, I decided to go to the information booth in the front of the station to inquire about my options.

"Sprechen Sie English, bitte?"

"Yes, a little" was the reply.

"I am urgently trying to get to the Hospital Universidad de Salzburg. Can you please tell me how to get there? It is an emergency!"

"Yes, you can take the number seventeen bus and get off at Oden-Platz, switch to the number four bus and it will take you there".

"Can I walk from here? How far is it?"

"It is about four kilometers that way". She pointed to the southwest and gave me some nebulous street names in broken English that meant absolutely nothing to me.

I decided to buy the bus tickets. The sun was high overhead now and blazing down on me. With my backpack it would take a while to walk there. I didn't believe I had any time to waste.

I stepped onto the bus and as I passed I asked the driver, "Hospital Universidad Salzburg, bitte?" while pointing down at the floor of the bus. He replied by shaking his head no and pointing at another bus.

I tried in vain to explain that I was told this bus would take me to the hospital but to no avail. He just pointed at the other bus again.

My shoulders slumped, I couldn't believe it. I traveled four thousand miles, hadn't slept in 3 days and I was finally here. But through a comedy of epic proportions, no one could reliably tell me where the hospital was or how to get there.

I got off the bus and went over to the other one. "Hospital Universidad Salzburg, bitte? I tried again.

The second driver shook his head and pointed back at the first bus.

I lost it.

"You have got to be fucking kidding me!" I exclaimed. He didn't understand me but it was clear I was more than a little agitated. After another shrug of his shoulders, I gave up and walked off the bus. I stood there exasperated and exhausted, trying to figure out my next move.

I had started panicking now, wiping the sweat off my forehead under my hat. It was stiflingly hot. I looked at the taxis again. "Shit". I looked at the buses and just shook my head in amazement at their indifference.

I remembered the young girl at the information booth pointing in the direction of the hospital. I stood in the blazing sun. The heat was burning through me like a torch. I took a deep breath and started walking in the direction she had pointed.

"Fuck it", I thought. I have come this far and I can make it the remainder of the way.

I'll just get there on my own. Salzburg can't be that big. I can walk three kilometers in a short time.

My walk started fairly crisp. Then as I started to picture Dad taking his last breaths and I hurried my pace a little, eventually breaking into a light jog. It suddenly became harder to see. My eyes were clouding over and my cheeks were starting to burn from the salt as tears started rolling down my face in the baking sun. I was exhausted and panicked. I couldn't get the thought of being too late, out of my mind. All I could picture was getting there and seeing his dead body. He needed me and I was too late. This was it. This was my worst fear. Just like with my Mom all over again. I felt an intense urgency to get to him right then.

"Please God, help me. I can't be too late."

My eyes were filled with tears now and my shirt was soaked with sweat.

My pace was as fast as I could run, the weight of my backpack slogging from side to side with every hurried step I made. It was a struggle but I pushed on as best as I could.

I criss-crossed through several side streets after leaving the station and then crossed the bridge over the Salzach River. I continued to try to work my way in what I believed was the general direction of the hospital.

After about five blocks of this, I realized that I was very lost and very tired.

"Hospital Salzburg, bitte?" I asked the first person I saw, gasping for air as I bent down and put my hands on my knees for support. The people on the street were very friendly and seemed to understand what I was looking for, they pointed me in the right direction in spite of my appearance and obvious distress.

I weaved through the streets and asked for directions several more times. Finally, after about thirty minutes, a nice older couple who spoke some English was able to tell me the hospital was just at the top of the hill to my left. I took several deep breaths, said thank you and started up the hill. I couldn't believe it. I was finally almost there.

The final hill proved to be more difficult than the streets below. I set out with everything that I had left, I was sprinting at this point. My lungs were burning, my legs were numb, I was dripping sweat as I ran, my head was pounding and I was praying out loud in gasps, "Please God. Please. Please let him be alive. Please God." I repeated over and over.

I was about a quarter mile up a steep hill and I had nothing left in my tank. I had to stop. I doubled over with my hands on my knees trying to catch my breath. As my lungs burned and legs ached, all I could think about was whatever pain I was feeling is nothing compared to what Dad is feeling and the fear he must be enduring.

Somehow, I had to find the strength to press on. One foot after another. Step by step. Take the next one. Take the next one. Ignore the sudden onset of shin splints burning like a flame all up and down my lower legs. Before I knew it, there was only about a hundred yards separating me from the hospital entrance. I took the final distance as fast as I could with all of the energy I had left.

After close to twenty hours of straight travel and almost three nights without sleep, I reached the top of the hill and rounded the corner to the entrance of the hospital. I made it! "I'm here dad," I muttered under my breath as I doubled over to try to catch my breath again.

CHAPTER 15

"Shit!" I said it out loud as I turned onto the hospital grounds. There must have been at least twenty buildings and none of them were marked. It wasn't obvious which building was the main entrance or admissions office. My urgency was at its peak now. I was frantic and exhausted and drenched in sweat.

I started asking everyone that walked by.

"Sprechen Sie English, bitte?"

"Yes, a little" was the standard response. Most people did not understand what I meant when I asked about the "admissions office". I did my best to explain that I was looking for the building that checks people in and out of the hospital. After several tries, I was directed to a three story brick building across the grounds.

I ran as fast as I could across the courtyard, up the steps and into the office. I couldn't feel my body anymore. I was in a daze from lack of sleep and I was experiencing an emotional overload.

All of the signs were in German but I was able to figure out that the admissions office was on the second floor. I flew up the stairs as fast as my exhausted legs could carry me. As I entered the office which was staffed with four women all working behind a counter looking very busy, I realized that I must look like hell. I was drenched in sweat, disheveled, gritty and had dark circles under my eyes from a lack of sleep. Judging from the strange looks I was getting, it was clear that my presence was somewhat shocking to them. I decided that now was not the time to be bashful.

"Hello, do you speak English?" I asked the first lady brave enough to greet me in my haggard state. I had decided to end the illusion of trying to speak German.

Her answer was no. Crap, I thought. She went and asked all of the other ladies if any of them spoke English. One of them said that they spoke just a little.

I took a deep breath. I was really about to lose it, feeling intensely emotional and still not sure if dad had made it through the night.

I began to explain slowly and calmly who I was, that I had been traveling all night from Colorado and that I needed to find out if my Dad was still alive. As I was speaking, it was clear that she was having difficulty understanding me. So I started over, explaining who I was and explaining that I was looking for a patient who was in the hospital. At this point my voice was starting to crack. I said Dad's name three times and spelled it for her. As she typed the name into her system, I held my breath. My heart was beating a mile a minute and the sweat continued to trickle down my back.

She looked up and said that she was sorry but she couldn't find him in the system. Fear stuck me in that moment; perhaps I was not even in the right hospital. Maybe there was more than one in Salzburg. I asked her if she could try again. This time, I got a pen and paper and wrote his name out clearly. M I C H A E L P E T E R S O N. As I handed her the paper, I looked into her eyes and in a desperate tone I said, "Please, I need to know if he is alive. I have traveled a very long way to get here for him. Please."

She nodded with compassion and finally seemed to understand.

She retyped his name in the system again. This time as she looked up, I could tell instantly that she found him.

"Oh, here it is. I see him!" she said with an air of

excitement and surprise.

I almost jumped up on the counter! I once again asked urgently and with a shaky voice, "Please! Is he still alive?" I could barely breathe as I choked the words out. I wasn't ready for the answer.

She squinted as she pressed another set of keys and read the screen. "Yes! Yes! He is alive!"

I fell down to one knee, held my head in my hands and completely lost it. The world started spinning and my vision started to close in on me. I was beginning to faint, while weeping from relief. I just couldn't hold it back anymore. The words, "Thank You God" kept rolling off my tongue in broken tones of emotion as I struggled to catch my breath. To hear that I had made it in time and was about to see him was such a relief, that I was overcome. He wasn't going to die alone.

Two of the workers, including my blessed broken English speaker rushed around the side of the desk in an effort to assist me. She asked me to sit, if I was OK, and if I needed a cup of water. I wasn't about to sit down now, not after the last two days of trying to get here. I told her I was OK, and stood up with shaky legs. As my head rush began to subside I asked her where he was.

"He is in the coronary intensive unit which is only three buildings away from here. Go out the door through the courtyard and it is the third building on your right. He is on the second floor."

Tearing for the door I looked back and yelled "thank you so much". I dried my eyes and nose on my soaked through shirt and started picking up my pace. This was it. I was finally here and I had almost gotten to him. I couldn't feel the pain in my shins or my exhaustion anymore. I felt alive and refreshed for having made it.

Running across the courtyard, I once again realized that I must look like absolute hell. I needed to change my clothes and get cleaned up but there was no time for that. As far as I knew, Dad could be taking his last breath at any minute.

Approaching the coronary care building I took the steps two and three at a time, threw the door open and ran up two flights of stairs to the second floor. At the top of the second floor landing I looked right and left. To the right was a long, dark hallway with linoleum tile floors with a white and orange checkered pattern. I could see many doors and a cafeteria with vending machines which would later become my home away from home. To the left was clearly the Coronary ICU, it had a secured door with an intercom system. I stood waiting and trying to decipher how to get in. I pressed the intercom button. Immediately, a man's voice came on and said, "hallo, wie kann ich Ihnen helfen?"

"Hello, do you speak any English?"

"Yes, a little", came the familiar reply. I was expecting it this time.

"Great. My name is Michael Peterson. I am here to see my father, he is in your ICU."

"Excuse me? I do not understand."

I was so close and just had one more door to get through, I was frustrated. I couldn't believe after all of this time, I was finally here and Dad was on the other side of this door. I was ready to lose it but I knew that I only had this one last hurdle to overcome. I took one more deep breath and a patience and calm came over me.

"I am here to see my Dad. His name is Dr. Michael Peterson. He is a patient here and ..."

He excitedly interrupted me and exclaimed, "Oh, yes, yes, yes! Hold on one moment, please!" The door buzzed and the lock clicked as it started to slowly open.

He came running down the hall with his hand extended and a smile on his face. "Welcome, we are so glad you are here. He really needs someone from the family to be here. Come this way, please."

I shook his hand and thanked him for his kindness.

"Right this way, please", he said again.

He led me down the hall and to the first door on the right. It was not a big room. There were six beds in it, three on each side. They each had pale blue curtains pulled halfway around the beds for privacy. As I turned into the room, I saw him right there in the first bed on the left. It was Dad. I made it. I have never been as happy as I was in that moment. I made it here for him.

His eyes lit up when he saw me. My heart skipped a beat and I got a little choked up. My eyes filled with tears ever so slightly. He looked very old, little, frail, tired and weak. But his eyes. His eyes were the same and when I saw them light up for me, it meant everything.

"You're here", he said in a tired voice, but it was still him. It was still Dad. I could tell right away.

"You made it! They told me you were coming", he said with a slight smile on his face. He seemed very relieved and thankful. I could tell he was happy to see me and it felt so good.

"You grew your hair long", he said with just a hint of bemused fatherly judgment.

I brushed it off, smiled back at him and told him that there was absolutely nothing that could have stopped me from getting to him. I told him that I was glad to see him and that I wasn't going to leave under any circumstances unless we left together. I gave him a quick, strong embrace.

He made a funny look at his hand as he felt my back and my sweat soaked shirt, but he smiled a smile of gratitude. I was so happy to be there and that he knew I came all this way for him. To have made it here in time to see his face and his relief was everything to me and everything that I wasn't able to do for Mom when her time had come. It felt so good, but I had no idea what to do next. I never even gave it a second of thought until now.

He looked like hell. His hair was a mess and he had a

salt and pepper beard that must have been a few days old. He was hooked up to multiple monitors and IV poles that each had tubes extending out of both arms.

The veins on his arms were a dark shade of black and blue from the needles. His skin was spotted by old age and he clearly had lost a good bit of weight. In spite of his grave condition, I could tell by looking into his eyes that it was still him. He hadn't lost his mind. It was a relief.

He had two huge bumps on his head. One over his left eye with what looked like fifteen to twenty stitches and one near his hairline at the top of his forehead with at least another ten stitches. The skin around each wound was purple and black.

"Dad, you look like someone kicked your ass", I smiled as I surveyed the considerable damage.

"I know, it feels like it too", he said with his old brand of sarcasm and humor.

"Does it hurt? Are you in pain?"

"No", he said with his signature shrug.

I knew he wouldn't tell me even if he was. It wasn't his style.

"Can I get you anything, Dad? Anything at all? Just say the word and I will figure it out."

"Yeah, you can get me the hell out of here", he barked with a hint of dark humor.

Dad spoke like the man I spent my life knowing, loving and looking up to. I have to admit, I was incredibly relieved that he seemed like himself. An old and tired version of himself but it was still him. In a brief moment of selfishness, I had been really worried about the mental state I would find him in. It would have made all of this so much more difficult if he wasn't his usual self.

"How are you feeling?" I asked him again after surveying him thoroughly.

"OK", was the reply with another shrug of his shoulders. He was typically a man of few words but I came a long way and wanted more than just an OK. I would have to work at it to pry more out of him.

"Does your head hurt?" God, it sure looked like it did. It was hard to look at.

"No, it's not too bad. It's my back. My back is killing me from laying in this bed for so long". He had been in that bed for over three weeks now, off and on.

Without a word, I immediately went over and helped him sit up. I turned him slightly to his left so I could start digging my thumbs and hands into the muscles in his back. I forgot all about how tired I was, I just wanted to give him some relief from the pain he was feeling. He didn't say anything but he was making noises that reflected the relief it was providing him.

When I was a young kid and even up through high school, he always used to have me walk on his back as he stretched across the ottoman in our family room. We used to watch whatever sports were on that night and I would walk on his back while we watched. It felt really good to help him.

"What are they telling you about your condition?" I asked.

"Nothing", he chortled, expressing some frustration and a true desire to know more about his condition. On some level, I was pretty certain he knew.

"From what I was told, your heart stopped twice and they resuscitated you, which has landed you in here for a second time. Do you remember any of it?"

"No. Nothing. I keep waking up here. I want to get up and move around but I'm pretty tired."

"Are you eating anything? Are you hungry? How is the food?"

"Blech!" He made a contorted face and shook his head as if to say that the food was less than remarkable.

I was ready and willing to spring into action.

"All right, well I am here now so that shit is over," I said with conviction and a smile. "Tell me what you want.

Anything! And I will go find it for you."

"No, that's ok. Why don't you sit down and relax. You look tired."

I had seen and heard this act before and I wasn't going to stand for it. "Look Dad", I said, "I have traveled for thirty hours from Boulder to be here with you and help you and that is exactly what I am going to do. Now, I am going to go get you something good to eat. You can either tell me what you want or I will just get you what looks good to me".

He gave me a sheepish smile, l knew he would love something good to eat but he didn't like to be put in his place by me. In the end, I knew he was grateful.

"How does a hamburger and a coke sound?" I posed.

"Like a blessing," he said with a wry little smile over his face.

I got goose bumps by just to being able to do something so simple but in his state it must have felt like everything. I would have gladly traveled all of this way any day of the week just to bring him a burger and a coke.

I helped him lie back down and get comfortable. I told him I was going on a recon mission to find the best freaking cheeseburger in Salzburg! I already knew how he liked it. His way was medium rare, with a tomato, raw onion and a little ketchup. I reached over, embraced him and told him I would be back in a flash. He patted my shoulder as we embraced as a way to say thank you and that he was very grateful that I was there.

On my way out I stopped at the front desk and introduced myself to the nurses on duty. They didn't speak very good English but they were very sweet to me and so very happy that Dad had someone here to love him and take care of him. I was a little overwhelmed by how they greeted me and how they were clearly caring for Dad in the toughest of possible circumstances. I tried to convey my thankfulness for the obviously high quality care they had been giving to Dad. It was quite touching, actually and on behalf of our entire family, I could not have been more grateful.

With that, I asked where the bathroom was and headed down the hall. I finally had a chance to change my clothes and clean up a little. This was a major event in my little journey. My clothes were so completely filthy. It was so nice to peel them off and put on clean everything. Unfortunately, I only brought one pair of shoes, so putting those back on was not pleasant but at least my socks were clean and dry. I felt like a new man and I was ready to set out on my mission to find Dad his burger and get back to him as fast as I could.

CHAPTER 16

Day 1. The cheeseburger, fries and Coke that I brought back from a restaurant only a few short blocks away was received very well. Dad was able to eat most of the burger and a few fries, or pommes frittes as they are called in German. The Coke must have tasted great to him because he drank the whole thing. His hands were shaky as he ate and I could see how weak he had become. It was hard to see him like this. He didn't say much but it was clear that he was grateful all the same. As he sat eating, the realization came over me that there had been such strong focus on getting to him and no thought of exactly how much work there was to do. The words "Now what?" kept ringing in my head.

First, I needed to meet with the doctors and get an assessment of Dad's situation and then figure out our next steps. All I knew is that they had said that his heart was very weak and he could die at any minute. It was hard to think about it now that I was here and looking him in the eye. I had to find out if there was anything we could do, anything at all.

I also needed to find a place to stay. I literally had not given it any thought at all up until this point. I needed to determine what Dad needed each day to make him more comfortable and to make the time pass. I had bought a book in the airport called the Reagan Diaries that I thought we could read together. Dad was one of the most voracious readers I have ever known and he was a big Ronald Reagan fan. I thought it would be a good choice for him. I would soon find that he was too weak to read on his own and that I was going to be reading out loud for hours on end.

Mostly, I just wanted to focus on keeping him company, making sure he was comfortable and getting him anything he needed. One of the nurses was kind enough to find me an old vinyl lawn chair, the kind we used to have in the seventies. It wasn't perfect but it did recline. I could lay back and doze, which would allow me to maximize the time I was able to spend by his side. That after all, was why I was here and I was very grateful for the consideration.

Before anything else, I was here to just be with Dad until the end, an end that neither of us wanted to face.

I sat down in my lawn chair and opened my laptop. The hospital had a wireless connection so I was able to get on line, send emails, read the news and stay connected with work.

I started with an email to get my international dialing on my blackberry set up ASAP. I marked it as urgent and got an almost immediate reply stating that it would be enabled by the end of the day. I would be able to brief Danny, Rich and Janet later that night. They would all be able to call me directly for updates or if they wanted speak to Dad. Also, I could work much more efficiently from Dad's bedside or the hotel or wherever I may be. I sent an email to all of them telling them a time that I could do a conference call to brief them on Dad's situation later that night. I told them to use my conference line at 10:00 PM Salzburg time, which was 3:00 PM in the East Coast and 2:00 PM in Michigan where Rich was.

Dad was clearly tired, but he wanted to stay awake. He had been alone in that bed for so long and now that I was here, he wanted to talk. After another back massage and conversation, I decided to open up my browser and check on some news sites to bring him up to speed on everything that had happened in the world since he had been laid up.

I read him updates on the upcoming Pittsburgh Steelers

training camp, free agent signings, and players they had lost. We had a good conversation about their chances for winning another Super Bowl and who else were contenders in the upcoming season. Once a Steelers fan, always a Steelers fan.

Dad had recently bought a large screen TV. He was talking about how amazing it was to watch the Steelers or any sports in high definition. It made me a little sad to think that he may not get the chance to get home to see just one more game on it. I pushed the thought out of my mind and didn't let on my growing concerns.

We talked for an hour or so and I could see his eyes getting heavy. I suggested that he take a nap while I used the time to go find a place to stay. He agreed. I went out into the hallway to meet the doctors and the people on the evening shift that had just arrived. I would get to know them all very well over the coming days. They brought the head of the department over to meet me. Her name was Dr. Klein. She must have been in her mid-fifties. She was a medium height lady with reddish brown hair. She didn't speak much English. She was very friendly and thanked me for coming. I tried to ask about Dad's condition but all she could convey was that he was very, very sick and not in good shape. I decided to let it go at that for the night and to find a way to have more of a conversation tomorrow.

As I quietly went back into the room to get my backpack before heading off to find a place to stay, I could see that Dad was already asleep. He looked so helpless, old and tired. I just stood there at the foot of the bed looking at him. I felt a wave of sorrow for the condition and position he was in and I started to silently pray for him to have peace and to not be in any pain or discomfort. This was so typical of me, a recovering Catholic, to turn to God in times of need and only in times of need.

As I stood there watching him, I noticed his blood pressure and his blood oxygen levels were dangerously low. It made me wonder how his heart could still be pumping after having given up twice already. It felt like it could end at any minute. I felt like every second was precious. But I knew he had to sleep so I reluctantly decided to leave.

On my way out, I gave the front desk my cell phone number and left instructions to call me if his condition changed. I was determined to be there if anything was going to happen. But first, I had to find a place to stay.

I wanted to make sure I stayed somewhere within walking distance to the hospital. I walked to the bus stop outside the hospital grounds and began looking at a map of the city. I could see that if I turned left on the main road and headed towards downtown Salzburg, I would have the best luck finding places to stay. Sure enough, after about 10 minutes of walking there was a Pension that had a "Rooms for rent" sign. It was a very traditional German chalet type house with dark wood paneling on the outside and flower boxes filled with red and white geraniums hanging from every window. It was very inviting. I decided to give it a try.

Once inside it was stiflingly hot with no air conditioning and only a small attic room left available. I decided I would take it due to its proximity to the hospital. I would suffer through the heat. I went downstairs to tell the owner but as I started asking the words, "Do you speak English," she told me that the room was just rented in broken English and she had no more vacancies.

The exhaustion was ready to take me at this point, but with no other choice I went back on to the street and kept walking towards town. I really had no preference between a hotel, a pension or even a hostel. I was starting to get a little worried when I walked more than a few miles and still hadn't found a place. After about three miles in the steamy evening air, I saw a pizza place called Pizza Mann that looked pretty inviting. I made a mental note of it for later and kept going. I didn't need pizza. I needed sleep.

Finally after another half mile or so, I found a larger hotel called the Hotel Neutor near Salzburg Zentrum and I didn't hesitate. I went straight in. It was on a major bus line and despite what I expected to be the exorbitant cost, it was perfect and still close enough to the hospital. It was about a three and a half mile walk to the hospital, or a 10 minute bus ride. I went straight to the front desk and asked if they spoke English, which of course they said, "Yes, a little."

When I asked if they had a room, to my relief, they said they had one room left but only for one night.

I told them I would take it and that I wanted to stay indefinitely. I was willing to move rooms each night if I had to. All I cared about was that I had a place to sleep, if only for a little while. It was almost time for me to pass out, so I would have paid anything.

As I expected, it was expensive.

The cost of the room per night was the equivalent of two hundred and seventy-five dollars. That could really add up depending on how long I was to be here. I would have given a kidney to be able to sleep right then so I hurriedly provided my credit card and passport. It could have been a thousand dollars a night and I think I still would have taken it. A few minutes later they handed me my room key, which was a real key like in the olden days. Without any hesitation, I was off to the grand staircase and up two flights of stairs taking them one slow step at a time. I was still feeling the sting in my shins as I climbed. On the second floor, I rounded the corner and made my way down a wide hallway, finally stopping in front of room two sixteen to my left. I took a huge sigh as I inserted the key and turned the lock. The door slowly creaked open like a pensive gateway to a forbidden hideaway.

The room was spacious, with a dark, mahogany antique coffee table in the middle. It had a separate toilet room and a large bathroom that had a tiny stand up shower which I was sure I would barely fit in. It was divided into two sections, with one section for sleeping and one section that would substitute as my office. It was not very remarkable or even comfortable as I would soon find out when I got on the bed. I didn't care at the moment. I threw my bag on the floor and made my way straight to the bed, peeling my clothes off as I approached and ultimately flopped down on top of it. I was too exhausted to pull the blankets down or even put a pillow under my head.

I was unconscious almost as soon as I hit the surface. After almost seventy two hours without any meaningful rest, my body was shutting down. I had made it. I had done what I came here to do, or so I thought. Now, after all that I had been through to be here for him, I felt the sweet release of sleep beginning to take me over. I contemplated with fear, what the next days would bring. My last thought as I drifted off from consciousness was the look of Dad's face as he enjoyed his cheeseburger. It felt good to be here for him. But I had no idea what lay ahead of us.

CHAPTER 17

Day 2. There was no alarm set but the various engine hums and horns honking during Wednesday morning rush hour woke me up around seven. My phone was on the dresser by the bed in case the hospital called. As soon as the traffic roused me, I checked my phone and was relieved to see that there were no calls that I missed while in my sleep-coma. I also checked to see if international dialing was indeed functioning. To my relief, it was. "I sure could have used that yesterday", I thought as I headed straight for the shower.

I decided to get up and get to the hospital early, I wanted to spend the morning with Dad. The shower in the room was about half of the size of a coat closet back home, however the water was hot so I let it flow over me for what felt like a long time. Washing away all of the grime and sweat from the last two days was a welcome blessing. I didn't want to take too long in case Dad was awake and waiting for me. Once dressed, I made my way to the front desk to get a bus schedule and to begin planning my day.

The buses ran like clock-work and it was quite easy to understand which bus to take to get to and from the hospital. My hotel was on the red line and the number 12, 42 and 17 buses all took me right by the hospital and then subsequently back to the hotel from the other side of the street. There didn't seem to be a lot of places to eat although there was that PizzaMann place along the way in the back of my mind.

As the bus rolled down the street, I checked for places of

interest along the way such as restaurants, bakeries, coffee shops and grocery stores. Dad was going to need some supplies and some creature comforts for sure.

I wanted to establish a daily routine as soon as possible so that Dad could feel some kind of "normalness", even though his situation was far from normal. His comfort was my main concern.

When the bus stopped near the hospital, I didn't go straight onto the campus. Instead I walked for several blocks in each direction to identify places I could get food, coffee or anything else he may need. I was starting to get a better feeling of my surroundings and was prepared to settle in for as long as we would both be here.

I stopped at a bakery and got Dad a coffee, he always drank his coffee black with nothing in it. I also got him a croissant with butter and jam, as well as a muffin. I thought it would be a nice departure from his normal morning fare. I got myself a muffin and some orange juice. With breakfast in hand I began to make my way back to the hospital to settle in for the day with Dad. I was also bringing him the book I had bought to help him pass the days.

I got there a few minutes later and got buzzed into the ICU without delay. Turning the corner and seeing him waiting for me was nice and sad at the same time. I felt so bad for him and wished I could do more. It was a reminder that this was not a normal visit between us and that he could literally die at any minute.

He was delighted at the sight of coffee and croissant but he needed help sitting up to receive them. It was becoming more apparent just how weak he had become.

I have to admit that when I arrived yesterday and saw how lucid he was and how he seemed to be his normal self, albeit very tired, that I took for granted just how grave his situation was. I made it a point to try to speak with the doctors today to see where he was and what could be done for him. I noticed his numbers on his monitors. I am not a doctor, but I knew what they meant. His blood pressure was 54 over 66, which was dangerously low and his ejection fraction was 23. This meant his heart was barely pumping and barely getting any oxygen to the starving cells of his body. It explained why he was so weak and tired.

He thanked me for the breakfast food and asked me to put butter and jam on his croissant, which of course I was happy to do.

His hands were shaking as he tried to eat. He was having trouble bringing his hand up to his mouth. It was hard to watch and almost more than I could take, but I kept silently reminding myself that this is precisely why I was here. He needed me. I put butter and jam on his next piece, took a deep breath then put the croissant up to his mouth and began feeding him.

He sort of had to look away as he chewed, I could tell he was feeling embarrassed. I think I was feeling it to.

He was the strongest man I had ever met in my life and here I was feeding him. It was very hard to take in. I swallowed down any emotions I had about it and kept feeding him until he was done. The image of his weakness was going to stay with me, that much I knew. I gave him a sip of his coffee every couple of bites.

As I watched his shaky hands try to hold his coffee cup I was transported back to a vivid memory when I was no more than six or seven years old. I had just been through another surgery on my mouth. I was feeling extra scared, extra self-conscious about the scar on my face and extra dependent on Dad.

I didn't want him to leave the house. In my six year old mind, I was scared of another needle in my leg, or worse, another gas mask over my face. The anesthesia made me sick for days each time I had an operation. Fighting against the doctors to get the mask off my face was one of my most traumatic childhood memories. Almost worse than the electricity itself. Almost, but not quite.

It was the height of summer. It must have been July or August. It was hot and humid, like all summers in Pennsylvania were. The nightly thunderstorms would produce a chorus of house-shuddering thunderous claps, one after the other as the storm would pass through.

On this particular mid-day there was a nasty storm. It was the kind where the sky opened up with torrential rain, the wind whipped at a fierce pace, and the thunder claps shook the house's foundation. I used to watch the storms from the kitchen window and guess how far away the lightning strikes were by counting the seconds between the lightning and the thunder. Our dog Max used to run and hide under the bed. The thunder really freaked him out. Although I was deathly afraid of electricity, I never feared lightning from thunderstorms like I did extension cords. I was fascinated by the lightning and loved to hear the thunder and feel it shake the house.

After this particular storm was over, I took my black Schwinn dirt-bike (the one with the banana seat and big motocross knobby wheels) out for a ride to survey the damage around the neighborhood. As I got about a block away from home, I saw what looked like a bird's nest on the ground by the big Oak tree beside the Watson's house. It was upside down. I reached down and turned it over, there were two halves of an empty egg shell inside the nest, but nothing else. "That poor little baby bird", I thought to myself. I wondered if a cat had gotten to it after the storm. I surveyed the grass around the tree for a few feet in each direction, but didn't see anything. As I was about to get back on my bike, I heard the faintest little chirp. I looked back by the base of the tree and I let out a gasp as I saw it. The little baby bird must have just been born, it looked so fragile, scared, and in trouble. I started talking to it like a little kid talks to an animal, asking it if it was OK and if it was hungry. He clearly couldn't fly yet and his mom was nowhere to be seen. I decided to do what any little kid would do. I gently picked it up, put it back in its nest and took it home. I pedaled my bike slow and careful as I held the nest in my left hand. As I pulled in to our carport I called out for my Mom to come quick.

I set the nest by the door and went inside to get my mom. She came out right away and met my bird with wondrous eyes and an audible "Awww!" Just then the little bird started chirping and raising a ruckus. I figured he must be hungry, and I am sure he was scared. Mom warned me that sometimes when a baby animal comes in contact with a human, the mommy bird might reject it. I was devastated at the thought. I didn't want anything like that to happen, so I vowed to protect him, feed him and to make sure he was OK. I decided to name him Ralph. I wouldn't leave his side

Dad got home from work shortly after and we set out together with a shovel to gather up some worms to feed to Ralph. We quickly caught four or five worms of various sizes thanks to the ground still being wet. Our garden shovel was easily able to sink into the earth down by the creek. Once we had the worms in a cup, Dad went inside to the medicine cabinet and took out an old bottle of eye drops, rinsed out the dropper and got a cup of water to give to Ralph.

Now we had to figure out how to get the worms and the water down Ralph's throat. Dad showed me how to feed him. He took one of the smaller worms and held it over Ralph's head like his Mom would do and waited for Ralph to open his beak. But Ralph didn't open his beak, he must have been too scared to eat. He just kept chirping.

I stayed on the carport for two hours trying to feed that bird. I dangled that worm back and forth over the bird's beak for what must have been a hundred times. I was so scared that Ralph was going to die any second if he didn't get some food. Meanwhile, Ralph's mom, a beautiful red cardinal was circling around the carport and even landed in the big tree at the edge of the driveway. She was chirping wildly. I couldn't tell if she was chirping for me to feed her baby or to back away so she could take care of him.

I was determined to nurture this little baby bird back to good health but I was getting tired and frustrated because no matter what I would do, I couldn't get Ralph to eat the worm.

Just when I was about to give up, Dad came back outside and asked to try again. He took the worm, held it over Ralph's head and dangled it there, moving it back and forth in front of his eyes. Finally, after hours of attempts, Ralph threw his head back and opened his beak as Dad gently lowered the worm into it. I think Ralph's hunger overtook his fear. We were so excited. It was my turn to try.

Dad showed me again how to do it and this time Ralph wasted no time at all, he devoured the second worm. Mom came out to join us and I showed her how to do it, Ralph threw back his third worm. It was time to give him some water, so I took the dropper at Dad's instruction and put 4 drops into his beak. He eagerly took it and opened up for more.

Dad put his hand on my shoulder and squeezed tight as if to say, great job. We were so excited and so happy that we were actually feeding this bird and saving his life. We debated what to do next for Ralph. We agreed that it wasn't reasonable for me to feed him and take care of him every day, but I was scared that Ralph's Mom was going to abandon him because of our human contact. Dad was certain that wasn't going to happen and thought we should put Ralph back in the nest and put the nest back in the tree. He mentioned that if his mom had been watching and chirping, she would probably take him back and take care of him. After a lot of convincing from Dad and Mom, I reluctantly agreed.

That night at dusk we said our good nights to Ralph and I gently put him back in the big tree at the end of the driveway. I promised him that I would check on him in the morning and I meant it too. I was worried about Ralph and I was sure that I would get hardly any sleep that night. After I put him back in the tree, I ran inside and sat in the bay window; watching to see if anything would happen. It couldn't have been more than two minutes before I saw mommy Cardinal fly right into that tree. She wasn't going to abandon her baby. She loved Ralph just like my Mom and Dad loved me. She wanted to be the one to care for him. I called to Mom and Dad to come see. We were all so happy. I felt so good to have helped that helpless little baby bird stay safe and get back to his mommy.

Seeing Dad so weakened reminded me of Ralph, the only difference was that I was the only one here to take care of him and protect him.

Once Dad was finished with his coffee and his croissant, I presented him with a newspaper and a book. The only paper I could get was a USA Today which is often light on sophisticated reporting, but was sufficient to provide an overview of the goings on at home and across the world.

The book I had brought for Dad was the "Reagan Diaries" which was a listing of all of Ronald Reagan's diary entries while he was in office as President for 8 years. I noticed that he was having trouble holding the book up and keeping it steady, so I offered to read it to him. His response was a reluctant yes. I can only imagine how depressing it was for him to be so weak as to not even be able to hold up a book. I kept remembering what the doctor's had said that he was very weak and that if someone from the family was going to come for him, it had to be now. He could literally die at any moment.

I pulled up my lawn chair close to the bed, propped my feet on the wheel base and turned to page. This was a scene that was to be repeated every morning and every evening for the next week and a half.

We read, talked, dozed and sat in silence for the entire day. When he got hungry, I went out to find him some-thing good to eat. For dinner, I brought back some Schnitzel and fries, which he seemed to enjoy although he didn't have much of an appetite. Feeding him remained one of the hardest things to do.

I left that night around eight in the evening and decided that I would walk back to the hotel to clear my head. I had several conference calls for work to attend to once I got back to my room so I decided to stop for some pizza and a beer on the way. The conference calls were mostly uneventful and I was able to handle everything that needed to be done for that day.

As I laid in bed later that night, I had trouble sleeping. All I could picture was how weak he had gotten and my mind wandered to the inevitable questions of "what next?" and "what else can I do for him?" The picture of him in my mind of being too weak to cut his schnitzel was troubling me and I wanted so much to be able to help him. It was a very helpless feeling.

After innumerable tosses and turns, sleep finally took me and I began a much needed few hours of rest. Tomorrow it would start all over again.

CHAPTER 18

Day three. There is no fucking Ginger Ale in Salzburg! I am certain of this!

We were now getting into a normal daily routine that included breakfast with coffee for Dad while I had orange juice. He would try to eat his croissant with butter and jam on his own when he could and if he couldn't, I would feed it to him. I would read the USA Today aloud for him and we would talk about the news, followed by anything on our minds.

While we had some nice discussions, there were no deep "meaning of life" talks. These were not your "Tuesdays with Morrie" kind of moments. I did my best to make sure to keep it that way too. Dad seemed to really believe that he was going to make it out of this and get back home. I wasn't about to say or do anything to change or challenge that. So instead of discussing life's most important lessons, we talked about the upcoming football season or his dog or what he was going to do when he got home.

When we would run out of topics to cover, I would pick up where we left off in the Reagan Diaries and read aloud until one of us started dozing off.

Dad would often doze off and take naps throughout the day. I had decided that while he slept, I would run some errands and find ways to make him more comfortable.

I had planned to buy him a CD player and some classical music CD's to drown out the sounds of the other patients. In one particularly sad case, there were noises coming from a man dying alone with no one but the medical staff by his side. I was thankful that didn't happen to Dad. I was hoping to bring him a little bit of calm and solace through some of his favorite music. After our morning routine I asked Dad if there was anything he wanted or needed before I set out to find the closest mall or electronics store, his reply seemed simple enough.

"You know what I would love? Some Ginger Ale!" His mouth was watering as he thought about it. I smiled and said, "You got it!" As kids, we would always drink Ginger Ale whenever we were sick or had an upset stomach. I have very fond memories of Mom and Dad going out to the store to get Ginger Ale whenever we had the flu or were feeling under the weather.

"Ginger Ale it is. I will be back in an hour or two. Sit tight!"

This shouldn't be too difficult, or so I thought.

Two and a half hours and twelve stops later, no one had even heard of Ginger Ale and most of the people I asked didn't speak much English, if any. I was growing more frustrated with every stop. There was a bakery or market where you can get snacks or sodas about every block or so in Salzburg. I went to all of them that I could. The conversation was always the same.

"Excuse me. Sprechen Sie English, bitte?"

"Yes, a little."

"Do you have any Ginger Ale?"

"Huh?"

I hated to let Dad down but I would not be returning with a Ginger Ale. I figured that the next best thing would be a Sprite. So I decided to buy him two of those instead on my way back.

I continued on to the bus stop. I had gotten broken directions from the hospital on which bus to take to get to the largest shopping mall in Salzburg. It was called Europark, and it was about twenty five minutes away by bus. I fell sound asleep just a few minutes into the ride. The lack of sleep, working at night, the stress of seeing Dad this way was all catching up on me.

I woke up somewhere clearly outside of downtown and walked up to ask the bus driver if I had missed the stop for Europark. He did not speak any English so I mentioned the name of the stop and he pointed off into the distance which I took as universal sign language for "it's coming up."

He announced the stop for Europark and I got off the bus. I noticed that it looked similar to a mall you might visit in Colorado or anywhere else. I had emptied my backpack that I had taken with me to pack anything I bought for Dad. I was ready to go.

I spent much of the next two hours walking through the mall, trying to find what I was looking for. Mainly, I wanted some nice soothing music and a music player, I also planned to get Dad some special pillows that would conform to his body in the hopes that it could alleviate some of his back pain.

First things first, I went to the electronics boutique and picked out a CD player and several CDs of classical music. I was astonished by how crowded the store was. I got into the checkout line and waited for what must have been twenty minutes. I asked the checkout clerk if they spoke any English and this time the answer was a curt, No!

I presented my credit card without any hesitation or notion that there might be a problem. The clerk handed my card back to me and told me something in German that I couldn't understand. There must have been ten people in line behind me impatiently staring at me, hoping I would get the hell out of their way.

The checkout line was very narrow. I couldn't go forward with the merchandise and I couldn't go back because the aisle was blocked by people. I tried both my VISA and

American Express, but she wouldn't take either. The other shoppers in line behind me were angrily beginning to switch to different check-out lines.

Finally, I handed my merchandise back over to the clerk, and motioned for them to let me out of the line and through the turnstile. They agreed and I slithered away, embarrassed and frustrated.

I figured out where I could find an ATM and got some cash. I had to take out around seven hundred euros to pay for everything that I wanted to get Dad. I proceeded back to the electronics boutique and picked up the CD player, a Mozart CD, a Wagner CD and a Tchaikovsky CD. I made sure to go to a different checkout lane this time and had an uneventful check-out experience by paying for everything in cash.

I made my way back to the bus stop with a backpack full of pillows, a soft cashmere blanket, a reading light, the CD player and the music. I also had several snacks and sweets that I thought he might like, although he never really had much of a sweet tooth. In all, I had spent around six hundred and fifty euros. On the way back to the hospital, I would stop and get him some Sprite and hope that it satisfied his craving for Ginger Ale. I really didn't want to disappoint him.

"You're packing a suitcase
For a place
None of us has been
A place that has to be believed
To be seen."

-Lyrics from Walk On, by U2

CHAPTER 19

Day four. The routine continued but now Dad had more comfortable pillows, a blanket, music, snacks and a nice lamp (in comparison to the overhead fluorescent lights). He was very appreciative of my efforts and the pillows seemed to help his back and neck right away. While we had settled into a nice routine, there was something different about this morning and I was dreading it. I had to find a way to communicate with the doctors and get an assessment of Dad's situation.

I got to the hospital early, at around 8am. I stopped at the bakery along the way and got Dad the same croissant with butter and jam; I got my usual orange juice. He was hungry, which I took as a good sign.

We sat for a while and talked about things going on at home. I was able to connect to the Internet and read him the news and most importantly, I read him the daily updates from the Steelers training camp notes. The camp had just started and there was an article about which positions were open for competition and reports from the practices.

Once we finished that, I opened up the Reagan Diaries and proceeded to read for as long as Dad wanted me to.

At about eleven o'clock we took a break while he dozed off for a quick nap. He still needed lots of naps and was running out of energy more quickly. I got back to my work and was able to get caught up on some emails . Then I dozed off until twelve-fifteen.

A short time later I was awakened by a soft touch on my shoulder from one of the nurses who then asked me to step into the hall. To my delight, there was a medical student from Illinois waiting for me. Her name was Dr. Mary Wilson and she was here doing her residency. I was so happy to be able to communicate freely with someone, I almost hugged her. She was a site for sore eyes.

She had been asked by Dad's doctors to come over from the oncology department to help translate for me. She let me know that the doctors wanted to meet with me at one o'clock in a small conference room adjacent to the ICU and asked if I could make that time. "Of course," I said. "I'll be there. And thank you so much for your help."

"It is my pleasure. I just want you to know that from what they told me, things don't sound very good. I'm sorry. I will be in the meeting to translate for you but I want you to call me on my mobile in case you need any help after that. OK? I know you are a long way from home."

I almost lost it as she handed me her card, but I was able to swallow it down and compose myself. I was beyond tired and strung out, but all I could think about was that Dad was slowly dying in the room across the hall. For someone to show me that kindness and compassion was unexpected, and I appreciated it more than she could possibly know.

"I will and thank you so much for your help and your kindness. I will see you at one o'clock."

I went back into Dad's room and sat back in my lawn chair. Dad was awake and asked where I went. "They found a doctor from Illinois to translate for me."

"What did they say?"

"I am going to meet with your doctors at 1:00 and the American doctor is going to translate for me. I will let you know what they say."

Dad nodded his head in acknowledgment, almost as if he was a little uninterested. Something inside me told me that he already knew what they were going to tell me. He was always quite matter of fact about his mortality and was a "just hit me with it" kind of guy. He used to talk very bluntly about not wanting to be on life support under any circumstances. He used to act tough and said when it was his time, so be it. But he wasn't talking so tough now. He was scared, and I knew it. It was difficult to see that fear in him. I wanted so much to be able to take it away.

I changed the subject back to football. We talked Steelers for a good hour. He gave me a lesson on the greats of old and we talked about how nasty the Steelers-Raiders games were way back when the Raiders were accused of putting Vaseline on the football to ruin the Steelers' grip. We laughed about that one. It was a nice time that reminded me of better days. Dad got tired again and dozed off while I got some work done and read my emails. The business was not slowing down no matter what was going on in Salzburg. I started drifting off again. I could only stay on alert for so long before exhaustion over took me, and it took me at about 12:35.

I wasn't asleep for very long, I jerked awake and realized that it was now ten minutes to one o'clock and time to go out in the hall and wait for the doctors. I didn't want them to come into Dad's room to get me. I didn't want him to know that the meeting was happening. I had hoped he would forget and be able to rest. I went into the bathroom and splashed cold water on my face and the back of my neck. I was not sleeping well at night and felt very tired, but it didn't take much for me to wake up for what would be one of the most important meetings of my life and one that might determine Dad's fate. I was concerned but I was pretty sure I knew what they were going to say.

I was sitting out in the hall when Dr. Wilson came walking towards me. I got up to greet her with a grim nod. She asked me to follow her to the meeting lounge down the hall. As we stepped in, I could see that there were two German speaking doctors waiting for us and on the table was a box of tissues. This was definitely not a good sign.

I decided to break the ice and speak first. I asked Dr. Mary to translate for me and I once again thanked them for the tremendous care they were giving to Dad and tried to convey to them how much I appreciated it. As she translated, both doctors nodded with understanding and gratitude. They replied back that it was their job and they were happy to do it for such nice people. It made me feel good, and then they began.

I wouldn't say that Dr. Karsey (the German doctor who took the lead) had a great bed side manner, but he was compassionate enough and was definitely the "hit you with it" kind of guy that Dad would have appreciated.

As he spoke in German Dr. Mary translated in real time, speaking softly to my left. I didn't take my eyes off of Dr, Karsey the entire time.

"Your father is very, very sick and he is going to die here. It is a miracle that he is even alive and breathing right now. His heart has failed twice, he was dead twice and it was very difficult to bring him back each time. I don't believe that we will be able to bring him back if his heart fails again, which it will. It is not a matter of if, but when. And it won't be long. His heart is pumping very little blood through his body and is weakening by the day. I am sorry to tell you this but he will never leave this hospital alive."

Dr. Karsey paused to let me take in all that he had said, especially the last part. Dr. Mary spoke very softly and compassionately as she uttered the last line and put her hand on my shoulder in a caring way. I was feeling a little choked up but I was determined to stay strong and hold it together. All I could think of was how in the hell was I going to tell dad this?

Out of instinct, I asked if I could take him home. The answer was an immediate no. We had a short discussion about it and they pointed out that he was too sick to travel and that they wouldn't want to take on the risk. So I gave up on the thought and decided to keep my focus on how to make Dad's final days as comfortable and peaceful as possible. I felt heart-broken.

In all, it was a pretty short conversation; it must have been over in about ten minutes. Before I got up Dr. Karsey stopped me to ask about heroic measures if Dad's heart should fail again.

I paused and thought about it, taking my time. I got up and paced the room back and forth before answering. This was gut-wrenching and my thoughts were focused on what he would want in this situation. I know that he had always talked tough but that was not the vibe I was getting from him now that he was in this situation. This was an excruciating decision for me but one that I suddenly felt resolute over. I hadn't had the talk about dying with him yet and until I did, I was not going to authorize a Do Not Resuscitate (DNR) order. I made it very clear that they were to use heroic measures to try to keep him alive at all costs until I said otherwise. We weren't going to take any chances.

I had my suspicions about what he would prefer and I followed my gut. In my heart, in my mind, I just knew he wanted to fight. I wasn't sure what for yet or if he had any fight left in him, but something was guiding me to keep him going for something. Something important and beyond me.

As I left the conference room Dr. Mary reiterated that I should call her if I needed anything at all. I thanked her and wandered aimlessly down the hall. I became lost in my thoughts as I sat on the bench in the hallway outside of the ICU. My thoughts turned to what I was going to say to him. Before I went back in there, I needed some time to think about what to tell him and how. I went for a short walk around the hospital grounds and through the adjacent park. As I walked like a zombie through the crowded sidewalks, I began drifting back to happier times.

I watched a group of people that must have been family members hugging goodbye and parting ways in the courtyard. My mind swept back to the many times that I left our house on Hastey Dr. in Harrisburg. Once I was old enough to drive, I must have pulled out of that driveway and driven up the street thousands of times. Whether it was heading off to school or a game, or back to college, it was always the same thing.

Dad would walk me to the car and give me a hug. He didn't always say anything but then again, he didn't have to. As I backed out into the street, he would have his arms folded and he would nod and smile, waiting for me to make eye contact. Then I would start up the street and he would be there standing on the side of the road, watching me pull away, giving me his signature finger point. I took it for granted for most of my life. Now it was incredibly important to me and I felt desperate to do something for him.

CHAPTER 20

After the doctors laid it out for me, I was distraught but I can't say I was unprepared. They didn't even really have to say it. I knew this was it and it didn't matter if we were ready or not.

It was getting later in the day and Dad was tired but he wanted to know what the doctors had told me. He asked the question with the unfamiliar innocence of a child, the trepidation of someone who knew and the hope of someone who still wanted to live. Keeping what was confirmed from him was going to be hard, but I thought quick on my feet and told him that they said his heart was weak but that he had started to get stronger before and it was possible that he could do it again. He nodded his head almost in indifference with a faraway look on his face. I could tell he really wanted to believe me, but he knew better.

After we talked for a while, he was convinced that if he could just get home to Harrisburg, he would recover and get back to his normal life. I knew this wasn't the case of course, but I wasn't about to tell him that. He knew he was helpless and that he had to rely on me. I suddenly felt a tremendous burden on my shoulders. They had just told me that he would never leave Salzburg or this hospital alive. I wasn't about to lay that on him because I knew he wasn't ready for it. I didn't want him to give up. I knew in my heart the right thing was to keep him going for as long as I could. Something was pushing me to keep him going. Beyond logic, beyond hope, I had to.

I looked him in the eye and said, "Dad. What do you want me to do for you? You name it and I will do it!" He pushed himself up off of the bed with his elbows so he could get closer to me. We locked eyes and he stared at me with conviction and complete lucidity as he said "Get me home." He paused for what seemed like an eternity and the silence felt like it weighed a hundred pounds. "I want to go home." In a way, I think we both knew that he was really saying was, "I don't want to die here. Take me home so I can spend my last days with my family." My emotions were roiling inside of me in that moment. It took a lot of strength that I didn't know I had to choke them down and not lose it.

"OK. That is what I am going to do. I am going to get you home. I will start figuring it out tonight and keep you informed every step of the way, OK?" Of course, I had no idea how I was going to do that.

"OK," he whispered breathlessly, it took every ounce of his remaining strength. He sighed and laid back down on the bed, he was exhausted.

There was clearly relief in his sigh. This is what he was hoping for. It was why he wanted one of us to come for him. This is why I was here. I was going to dive in with all that I had to try to make his final request a reality.

I had no idea how I was going to do it. They had already told me that it wasn't possible. I knew it wasn't going to be easy, maybe even impossible. But I didn't want to let him down again. Not now. This was bigger than not finding a damn Ginger Ale. They told me he was too weak to travel and that he would never make it. I was determined to try, and I knew he was determined too.

"You look tired. Why don't you go back to the hotel and get some rest? I am going to sleep now anyway. I'll see you tomorrow."

"Are you sure? I don't mind staying while you sleep?"

I was so exhausted. I appreciated that in his state, he couldn't help being my dad. He was still worried about me and wanted to take care of me. It was amazing, and it made me proud of him and proud to be his son. I ran my hands through my hair as I considered what to do; I noticed a light rain starting to softly pelt the window.

"No. You need rest. You have been through a lot. You must be tired. I'll be fine and I will see you in the morning. Now go" he said with his old forceful, in-charge tone. I knew he was right. So I gave him a hug and he gave me the finger point and I left. Even flat on his back on his deathbed, it still told me all I needed to know and hear. I appreciated it now more than ever.

I don't remember leaving his room but somehow I made it to the bus stop. While I was waiting for the bus to take me back to the hotel, I sat and gazed off into space. I needed help and I felt completely alone.

As I was frozen there, neither in sleep nor in full consciousness, my mind drifted to the thought that maybe I could get him home. Then what? What would it be like for him once he was out of here? How would he feel once he was home? Could he possibly recover? Would he tell everyone I got him out of here? Would he tell everyone everything I did for him? Would anyone ever know? Would he even realize what I went through to get him home? I don't know why this was suddenly important for me. I wasn't here for any reason other than him. But still, it was hard and I was exhausted and emotionally overdrawn, I guess I needed someone to notice and someone to care. I could deal with it as long as I helped dad get home. I could push through as long as I could see him leave this life with dignity and on his terms. It would all be worth it and I didn't need anyone else but him to tell me it was all right and that I did good.

I felt an immediate pang of guilt for even allowing these types of selfish thoughts into my mind. How could I make this about me while he was laying there dying and helpless? This wasn't the first time or the last time I struggled with these thoughts. As much as I was happy to be there for him, I was still trying to deal with my own issues as much as I could.

I don't remember the bus pulling up and I don't remember it pulling on to the road back to the hotel. All I remember is the rain. This was not your run of the mill rain. This was now an epic summer downpour with raindrops the size of marbles. It was the type of rain where the sky opens up and pours down from the heavens, soaking and cleansing all that are willing to brave it.

The streets were quickly flooding. Rain like this reminded me of summer storms back home. It took me back to childhood days in simpler times with simpler ideals when all that mattered was the love of my parents and being a kid.

I'm not sure how but somehow my autopilot got me off the bus at my hotel.

When I stepped off the bus, it was really coming down. The massive raindrops were splashing in the newly formed puddles on the street and sidewalks. It was hard to tell if the rain was falling up or falling down. I walked up the stairs and through the familiar lobby and made it up to my room.

While sitting on the edge of my bed, listening to the rain pummel the window, my mind started racing. Dad, work, Megan, marriage, divorce, the kids, work again, the kids again after that, what am I going to do about my life?, Who am I?, What do I believe? How am I going to do this? Hoping Dad didn't die in the night, money, work again, Dad again and again. Suddenly I couldn't take it anymore. I had two hours before my next work call and I had to do something. I felt like I was going to explode. I got up and changed into my running shorts, a t-shirt, my running shoes and a pair of black running socks. I put my iPod in to a plastic bag and then I put the headphones in my ears and made my way down the stairs to the lobby. In no time at all, I found myself on the front steps under the overhang, just out of the rain. I looked out at Salzburg and took it all in.

Up until this moment, I hadn't fully realized how beautiful it really was. I was so caught up in my mission to get to Dad that I didn't really notice how incredible this place was. It was stunning, lit up at night with a soft glow from the rain and the low hanging clouds. It transports you back to another time. In that moment, I felt as if this was the one place in the world I was supposed to be.

It was magical and intoxicating. I took another moment to breath and take it all in. It was an amazing experience and one that I will always remember. What a strange time to have a moment like this. All of a sudden, I didn't feel alone, it was as if there was someone else there with me. I had never felt a presence like I did at that moment. It was comforting and peaceful.

The night was humid and the rain continued in a steady pour, showing no signs of letting up, but I didn't care. The streets were almost completely empty of traffic, the occasional person scurrying by under the cover of an umbrella or under a coat draped over their head.

Salzburg has approximately one hundred and fifty thousand people in it. But on this night, it was mine and mine alone. It was as if it was waiting for me to hand myself over to it, and I was ready to.

I descended down onto the street. I was soaked in seconds. The rain was warm but my skin was tingling with goose bumps and I felt a slight chill. All at once I felt rejuvenated by the rain, cleansed of my burden, unable to think of anything but the rain engulfing me as I looked up and surrendered myself to it completely.

I walked to the corner and took up a position under the cover of a tree where I started stretching my legs. I listened to the rain splashing down all around me. It was like standing next to a running shower. I didn't want it to end.

My thoughts drifted to Dad. I wondered if he was asleep yet. I hoped he was. I hoped he was able to get some rest. He had a lot ahead of him. It was comforting to me that he knew I was here for him. I had no idea how much time had gone by but I had finished preparing myself for the most exhilarating and freeing run of my life. I turned my MP3 player on and put it on Shuffle play.

I have always found that music can magnify whatever I was feeling at any given point in time. A specific tune, a certain lyric, a refreshing melody, could encapsulate my dreams, fears, desires and amplify them five hundred times. It could be any mood. It could be a melancholy song for a melancholy mood. Or a driving song for a desperate fight, or a triumphant song to celebrate the good times or a nostalgic song to celebrate all that we love.

My senses had suddenly come alive and every fiber of my being was on fire and alert. I took in everything around me, almost as if I was part of the city, part of its energy. It was overwhelming and as the music began, I could feel it magnifying. The feeling that I was not alone continued to grow stronger. The best way I can describe it is that something felt familiar, comforting and accepting. All I had to do was focus and connect to it.

As I hit the street and starting jogging towards the center of Salzburg, the first song to play on my iPod was the unforgettable song Kite by U2. It was a song written by a son for his dying father. I thought it was uncanny in its appropriateness as the haunting melody of the organ preempted the Edge's tearful slide guitar. As it rang in my ears my footsteps started driving in sync with the bass as the words began.

"Something. Is about to give. I can feel it coming. I think I know what it is.

I'm not afraid to die. I'm not afraid to live. And When I'm flat on my back, I hope to feel like I did."

It was 10:30 when I first started out into the rain. I was completely soaked by the time I got to the first corner and I didn't care the slightest bit. My breathing was erratic and not yet steady into the rhythm of the song, the rhythm of the night or the rhythm of my racing heart.

This was the most refreshing feeling I had had in a long

time. I felt free. I also felt scared, overwhelmed and just the slightest bit overcome. As each car streamed by in each direction and as each person scurried to get out of the rain, I became oblivious to them. I was alone in my thoughts, in my pain and my need for escape. I wanted more. I wanted to be alone with the rain.

I headed through a tunnel and was now only a few blocks from downtown. I ran up the cobblestone streets of the lamplight district and turned left down the alleys towards the main square and beer gardens.

"And hardness. It sets in. You need some protection. The thinner the skin."

I could feel the shin splints coming again but I knew I was going to push through it. My breathing had now settled into a regular rhythm and my legs would be numb soon, a sure sign that a good run was on the way. I kept telling myself that nothing was going to stop me tonight.

With each step I pictured him falling in slow motion and hitting his head on that cobblestone street. I saw him in his ICU bed too weak to eat. I had visions of him lying in his casket, dead. I told myself to keep pushing. Keep pushing for him. Help him out of this. You can do it. Find a way!

"I want you to know, that you don't need me anymore. I want you to know, you don't need anyone or any-thing at all."

As the chorus began to play, my skin stood on end and I had chills go up and down my drenched body. That's when I looked up and saw it. I stopped cold because I knew where I was heading and what I was going to do. I knew where I had to go.

"Who's to say where the wind will take you. Who's to say what it is will break you? I don't know which way the wind will blow"

"Who's to know when the time has come around? I don't want to see you cry. I know that this is not goodbye."

Hohensalzburg Castle began construction in 1077 and towers twelve hundred feet above Salzburg. It is one of the largest fortress castles in the world. It majestically dominates the Salzburg skyline and is an awe inspiring site, especially at night and especially on a night like tonight. It was my target at the moment and all of my focus was now on it.

As I turned the corner and saw the flood lights on the beautiful old castle, I knew that I had to get to it. Maybe the answers were up there. Maybe it had nothing at all to do with what was going to happen to Dad but I was determined to find out. I had made up my mind, this was life or death and it wasn't my life that was at stake. I had to get to it. Maybe if I did, just maybe, I could figure out what to do for him. I was trying to talk to God. I asked God to make a deal with me. If I get to the top of that mountain, let me get Dad back home alive. That's the deal! What do you say? I kept saying it over and over. What do you say? What do you say? Let's do it, I yelled as I started off on a sprint toward the base of the mountain.

"I'm a man. I'm not a child. A man who sees, the shadow behind your eyes."

It was as if the words of this song were written for me and I was captivated by them

The tears that began streaming down my cheeks blended with the rain and fell to the ground to become part of this place forever.

I didn't want it to end. The song, this run, this rain, this moment, this night. In spite of the fear and pain I was feeling, I wanted to stay in this moment forever.

I made one more left turn to head through the park grounds at the base of the mountain. I had at least another two miles to go to reach the top and it was all up hill on a switchback, cobblestone road. My shins were screaming again, my legs were feeling heavy and my shoes were completely soaked. The rain continued to pound down on me. After another mile, I was starting to get tired and the runner's high that had carried me this far was beginning to wane in spite of the surrounding magic and inspiration. But I was determined to keep my part of the deal with God and get to the top.

Twenty minutes later and I was really laboring. I lost track of the music, It was just background noise now. I was losing the inspiration I had felt and all I could feel was the burning in my lungs and the pain in my legs. Still I kept on pushing.

After what seemed like forever, I started to turn on what would be the final switchback before reaching the top. I started to pick up my pace. I was actually going to make it. I ran past the entry gate to the Castle grounds and began turning to my right. I was feeling fatigued, my exhaustion and my cluttered mind were catching up with me and distracting me.

My right foot hit a wet cobblestone that was sticking up slightly out of the road. The sole of running shoe could not grasp the edge of the stone and as I tried to turn, my foot slipped. My leg slid underneath me and my body became airborne and parallel to the ground for what seemed like forever.

My right knee and shin hit the ground first, my momentum made me roll over at least three times. I slipped off of the road and over the low rod iron fence and into the shrubs on the side of the road.

As I came to a stop amidst the trees and shrubs, I felt an intense pain in my right knee and shin. The run of my life and my deal with God had come to a sudden end. I wasn't going to save Dad at the top of the castle tonight. I had failed again.

It was over. My knee and shin screamed in pain and was pooling blood rapidly. I couldn't tell if it was serious or superficial, if I could go on or if I would need assistance back down the mountain. My chest was heaving as I tried to catch my breath. The MP3 player took a direct hit underneath me between my hip and the road, it was cracked and had stopped working.

I laid there in the shrubs for what must have been several minutes and I caught my breath. I didn't even look down at my leg. I didn't want to know. I didn't care. I felt like a failure, like Dad was counting on me and I let him down. I wanted to move but my leg was numb and I wasn't sure if I could.

The rain continued to pelt me. My mind swirled. Was this it? Was this all I had for Dad? My lack of sleep, my emotional overloads, my marriage falling apart and my own need for meaning all hit me while I was laying in those shrubs. In the end, my thoughts returned to Dad. He needed me. I didn't want to let him down. I felt completely alone and asked God for something. Anything. Give me a sign. Help me.

There was no sound other than the rain splashing around me. There were no trumpets or visions of angels and there was nothing overly obvious. But there was something. I felt it. It was as if there was something answering my desperate plea for help. It felt as if I was being engulfed in the rain and the shrubs and all of my surroundings. I could actually feel the energy all around me. I knew I wasn't alone in that moment.

At that point, I sat up. After catching my bearings for a few minutes I picked up my broken MP3 player and although I couldn't read anything on the display anymore, I pressed the play button. To my surprise, my broken music player began playing again.

As the tambourine started and the song "Walk On" by U2 began, I was reassured that I wasn't alone. Somehow I found the will and the strength and I began pulling myself out of the shrubs.

"And Love. It's not an easy thing. The only baggage that you can bring. Love's not an easy thing, the only baggage you can bring is all that you can't leave behind..."

As the song progressed into a melodic explosion, I felt my strength returning. I leapt up out of the flower bed and began pushing forward in a slow, gimpy gallop. My knee and shin were completely numb and there was a steady flow of blood running down my leg.

I was going to reach the top of that fucking mountain and nothing was going to stop me now. I couldn't feel my leg, but I didn't care. My elbows were both burning from their scrapes and I had a huge bump on my head that was trickling blood down the side of my face. It didn't matter, I wasn't going to let Dad down. If this was a metaphor for my life, for his life, I wasn't going to quit no matter what.

"And if the darkness is to keep us apart, and if the daylight feels like it's a long way off."

Once again, I was certain that this song was written and delivered to me for this moment in time and I wasn't just hearing it, I was feeling it in every fiber of my being and it was driving me up that mountain.

"Walk on. Walk on. What you got you can't see it and no one can ever steal it. Walk on. Walk on. Stay safe to-night."

"Your packing a suitcase for a place, none of us has been. A place that has to be believed to be seen."

I was into it now and was able to ignore the intense pain in my leg, I couldn't feel it anymore. I couldn't feel my body. All I could see was dad. All I could feel was the rain. I started running faster and faster, breaking for the top of the hill. The city with its lights reflected back down off of the low hanging fog. It was breath-taking and surreal.

Finally, I reached the top of the hill, exhausted, out of breath, bloodied, and numb. I fell to my knees and reached out to the heavens while the rain engulfed me and the song echoed in my head.

"And I know it aches how your heart it breaks, you can only take so much. Walk On."

"I did it. I did it. Thank You God!" As I spoke to God, for the first time in my life, I could actually feel an overwhelming presence speaking back to me and guiding me. Reaffirming that my path was right. It was unlike anything I had ever felt before or since.

That MP3 player never played another song.

In all my life, I had never felt closer to something beyond me than I did in that moment. I have thought about it thousands of times since and I keep coming back to the conclusion that I was not alone on that mountain that night and that something was looking out for me and for dad. All I had to do was listen.

The walk back down the mountain was long, wet and quiet. I contemplated all that I had felt and heard, in what was the most awakening experience of my life. When I got back to my room, I felt rejuvenated. I immediately opened my computer and did a search for "transporting critically ill patients overseas," I couldn't believe my eyes at all the results. This was going to take a while. I didn't sleep at all that night. By morning, I thought that I may have found a way to get dad home!

CHAPTER 21

The next three days were a blurry combination of our daily routine, classical music, take-out food and late night research. I was furiously searching to find a way to get Dad home. I must have made dozens of phone calls within the first eight hours. The hospital staff let me use a break room down the hall that was mostly empty so I wouldn't disturb Dad or the other patients. Even though I was told it was not an option, I started with the airlines. First Lufthansa, then United and Delta. Their responses were all the same. They did not carry the equipment necessary to care for Dad and they would not have any doctors on board in case something went wrong. It was just too risky. I quickly narrowed my focus to air ambulances. These were private jets equipped with fully certified doctors and nurses to care for the critically ill in a private environment while transporting them across the world. It was basically a flying ICU. This seemed like the perfect option but it was incredibly expensive.

I consulted with the U.S. State Department on reputable, registered international air ambulance services and created a list of companies that offered the service we needed. I started calling all of them. After an entire day on the phone I was able to find three viable options. My first condition for choosing the right one was how soon they could get to Salzburg, and how soon they could get Dad home. I knew in my heart that we didn't have a lot of time left. As I made the necessary calls and narrowed down my options, I had an overwhelming feeling that I was doing what I was supposed to do.

Of the many calls I made, I placed several to Dad's accountant. We didn't know his phone number but we knew his name and it didn't take long for me to find him. Dad was not exactly financially aware, and he had entrusted his accountant with the savings he had accumulated after he put all four of his kids through college. I can't say that he did a great job for Mom and Dad, but I was relieved that there were some funds available now when he needed them the most. When I reached him, he was very sorry to hear about Dad's plight and vowed to do everything he could to help. He remarked what a nice man Dad was and that he was keeping him in his prayers.

I got Dad to sign several forms, transferring power of attorney to me so that I could use his funds as needed to get him home. When I got into Dad's accounts, I found out that he had almost eighty thousand dollars that I could pull from. At the point he was at, Dad was willing to pay whatever it took. It was my job to find the most affordable, rapid transport possible and I was committed to doing just that.

I spent what must have been hours on the phone with Dad's health insurance company, explaining the situation and seeing how much of the cost of his stay in Salzburg and the trip home they would cover. It was not easy to get answers but I stayed persistent. The good news was that most of the hospital costs would be reimbursable but we would have to front the money and then make a claim.

I had gotten an estimate from the billing office at the hospital. Dad's care was approaching fifty thousand dollars. I almost lost my breath when I heard that. The insurance company decided to cover the cost of his hospital stay but they made it clear that they would not reimburse any cost associated with the air ambulance.

After contacting more the three different air ambulance services, I narrowed it down to one. It was called Air Health One and a quick check with the U.S. State Department showed me it was a legitimate and reliable. They also had many references that I checked out which made me more comfortable. The main reason I had settled on Air Health One was because it was currently on its way from Florida to Greece. They could make the turn from Greece and be in Salzburg in three days. The other services I contacted would require at least a week to get there and I felt that Dad did not have that much time. The only problem was the ridiculous path they would have to take to get him to Harrisburg. It would cost us twenty-nine thousand dollars up front. I almost fell over when they gave me the quote. I told them I would get back to them within the hour.

At this point I had been going non-stop and I was ready to drop. I made the occasional calls to Megan and the kids when I could. I could hear it in my kid's voices each time that I spoke to them, they missed me and I missed them. It was definitely time to go home. I called Danny to discuss the cost of the air ambulance and we both agreed it was expensive but that it was Dad's money and we would leave the choice up to him. They had also informed me that I was not able to join Dad on the flight because the Lear jet would be filled with equipment and there was no space on board for any family. This was distressing to me but I soon found out that this was the case with every private carrier.

After three days of research and too many phone calls to count, I walked in to Dad's room to present him with what I had found. I had used the hotel's business center to print wire transfer forms for the Air Health One bank accounts. The conversation was a relatively easy one until I informed Dad that they would only take him if he was sedated and intubated with a breathing tube the entire time.

He didn't like it but when I told him that it was non-negotiable, he reluctantly agreed. We both knew the implications of a breathing tube. It would be that much harder breathe on his own after such a long period of time once he was home.

He wasn't worried about the money and readily signed

the forms to transfer the cash and set the plan in motion. I rushed back to the hotel and faxed the forms to Air Health One and received their confirmation and flight itinerary shortly after. It all seemed so crazy and unbelievable but once I sent that wire transfer, it was all real and about to happen. I passed on the estimated arrival window to Janet, Rich and Danny so they could be there when Dad arrived.

It was Friday afternoon and the plane would be arriving late in the day on Monday. Dad then had to get through three more days before the jet arrived in Salzburg. I was praying he could hold out for that long. He was slipping away slowly, day by day. His vitals were holding steady but he seemed much less talkative. He did seem a little more at peace knowing that he was going to be heading home. I had already decided that I was not going to leave his side for those final days and would just sleep in the lawn chair next to him.

I needed to make what might be my last three days with him as comfortable and easy for him as possible, and that was what I planned to do no matter what it took out of me. I called Danny and Megan to discuss the plan and check in with the kids for a short while before arranging my return flight back to on Tuesday morning. I got back to my lawn chair at Dad's side around eight o'clock and immediately fell into a deep sleep.

CHAPTER 22

It was Saturday morning and the air ambulance was two days away now. I was, as usual, sitting in the lawn chair to dad's right. This time I brought him eggs and bacon with coffee. He didn't seem to have an appetite anymore but he was appreciative all the same. I was happy to do it for him. I was concerned that he was not able or willing to eat anything. He slept most of each day now and always seemed tired. After the events of last week, knowing that the Lear jet would be here in two days gave me some peace. I just hoped that he would make it that long. All he had to do was hold on. I also had a sprite in ice in the cooler for him for lunch when he was ready. I cursed Ginger Ale silently under my breath over and over each time I looked at the Sprite.

I was doing my best to stick to our daily rhythm and to keep him company. We were surviving, barely, even though we were both exhausted to the point of collapse. I continued to monitor his vital signs and his blood oxygen levels as usual and they all seemed to be holding steady for the moment. I read the Reagan Diaries for about 45 minutes and we discussed it for a little while, until he decided to take a break for a bit and close his eyes. I decided to take this time to use the bathroom, and go for a quick walk in the park before trying to make some phone calls for work.

While I was sitting in the park, I decided to make some personal calls. One to Megan, one to Danny and one to Dad's accountant to discuss his finances. I had a plan to liquidate some of Dad's securities so that we could pay the hospital.

While I was on the phone, the sky quickly changed from sunny to overcast. And just like that it started to rain.

I headed inside and dried off. I had brought a semi-clean shirt in my backpack so I changed as well. I got back into my lawn chair and pulled out my laptop to do some emails and review a contract I had to have marked up before the end of the day.

It was close to three in the afternoon now and I was feeling fatigued and a little unsettled. It was so dark from the overcast sky that it seemed much later than it actually was. I had dozed off for a bit and was half conscious when I noticed dad acting strange in the corner of my eye. He had the blankets pulled up to his chin and he was holding the edges like they were a life raft and he was drifting at sea. He looked like a scared child who just had a nightmare or who had just seen a ghost. He was staring up at the ceiling with his eyebrows furrowed and his mouth open. I quietly laid my laptop on the floor by the nightstand and stepped to the side of his bed.

"What is it, Dad?" I spoke softly.

"Do you see that?" he replied.

"See what?"

"You can't see THAT!?" he said, nodding toward the ceiling.

"No, Dad. What is it?"

"She has been up there staring at me all day."

I felt a cold chill sweep through my body at that moment, putting me on edge and making me more than a little uneasy. I was looking right where he pointed and all I could see was the ceiling. But when I looked at his face he was clearly seeing something that I couldn't. I had always heard about people having angelic visions when they were near death. It always creeped me out, and I never really bought into it. I had always believed that people's visions were made up in their minds. If I couldn't see it, it wasn't real, or so I thought until my recent experience at the castle. Looking at his face, I could see that this was as real as it gets to him. We were just discussing Ronald Reagan's presidency 45 minutes ago and he was able to remember every detail of the Iran contra scandal and the Oliver North hearings. Did he suddenly lose his mind? It sure didn't seem like it.

When I was very little I heard the story of how my Pop Pop had seen the Virgin Mary three days before he died. I always believed it as a kid, and that memory was not lost on me now. As I grew older, I had more and more trouble believing it, instead I viewed it as an old ghost story. As with all of my search for spiritual truth, there was never any proof and I didn't believe in ghost stories.

But now Dad was clearly seeing something. I was there staring at him and I know that it wasn't just in his mind.

He saw it. This was really happening.

"Who is it Dad?" I asked again. I wasn't ready for his response.

"The Vulture Lady." He paused. I was dead silent and couldn't find any words. I was frozen.

"You mean you can't see it?" He asked but never took his gaze away from the ceiling.

Another cold shiver went down my spine and my skin rippled with goose bumps. I was listening, but not necessarily hearing or registering what was going on. My head was spinning as I wondered, could this be real? Maybe it was my mind playing tricks on me but now I could feel a presence and it was very unnerving. It felt dark and sinister. I suddenly felt sick to my stomach, like I was going to throw up.

"No dad. I can't," was all I was able to get out. There was a long pause. I was speechless.

"Tell me what she looks like," I managed to say.

I was afraid and I wasn't sure why. Was this the rumblings of an old man losing his mind? And if so, then why was my Dad seeing an image of a Vulture Lady, rather than a nurturing angel telling him to not be afraid? I could really feel darkness in the room, even though I couldn't see it. I wanted to protect him as he began to describe what she looked like.

She was wearing a black cape with a black hood over her head. He could just barely see her face through the shadows.

She had pock marks and scars all over and her skin was worn, dull and gray. Her hands were under her chin. She had pale, bony fingers with long sharp claws for fingernails. Her eyes were sunken, narrow and black, empty and cold.

Her head was oblong and she had a long pointed nose and a long pointed chin. He could see her sharp teeth. She was smiling and laughing at him which made Dad as pissed off as he was scared.

"She's been up there all morning," he said to my surprise.

I was still speechless and frightened.

"Now she is pointing at me and laughing, beckoning me with her finger."

My instinct was to protect him, but how? What could I possibly do? This was beyond me. This was beyond flesh. This is the closest thing I could imagine to spiritual proof. What he was seeing and experiencing was real but it was evil, cold and dark.

Dad cried out, "Why don't you leave me alone?". The nurses' heads turned at the sound of his shriek but they didn't speak English very well and quickly went back to their work. Maybe they had seen this before. I know I hadn't.

I stayed by his side and tried to stay strong and supportive. Dad was mumbling something under his breath. He seemed to be telling her something, or maybe he was praying. When I asked him what he said, he just shook his head.

At this point, with no other options, I remembered the

feeling I had on the mountain. The feeling of guidance and of love. I gave myself over to it and did the only thing I knew to do. I began to pray for Dad and for his soul. I started to say the "Our Father" silently at first and then in a quiet whisper. By the end of it I was saying it out load.

"Our Father, who art in heaven.
Hallowed be thy name.
Thy kingdom come
Thy will be done.
On earth as it is in heaven.
Give us this day our daily bread
And forgive us our trespasses.
As we forgive those who trespass against us.
And lead us not into temptation
But deliver us from evil."

As I finished, I asked God to watch over Dad and protect him and I repeated the "deliver us from evil" line. I really hadn't expected to encounter anything like this and I was almost paralyzed with fear. I didn't want Dad to be afraid and I sure didn't want him being harassed by demons, real or imagined.

"Go away!" dad exclaimed one last time.

We were both motionless for a few minutes as Dad continued to stare upward. After a while, he seemed to relax a bit, his body less rigid.

"Did she leave, dad?"

"Yeah...She's gone."

There was more than a moment of awkward silence. Neither of us knew what to say.

"I hope she doesn't come back. Let me know if she does, OK?"

"OK. I'm tired and I am going to take a nap."

"OK, Dad. I'll be right here. As always. I will be right here. You let me know if you need anything." He didn't say anything, he just turned his head to the side and closed his eyes. I think he was as unnerved as I was.

I still had the goose bumps and chills. It was going to be a long night with little sleep.

I was there to care for him and to protect him, but I had no idea how to protect him from what just happened so I kept praying. I asked God to protect him and to give me the strength I needed to get him through this and to get him home. I was scared for him and I just wanted him to be OK.

I tossed and turned in the lawn chair for several hours, unable to do anymore work as I tried to come to grips with all that had happened.

Dad woke up around ten that night. He had to go to the bathroom and took one look at me and suggested strongly that I go back to the hotel to get some sleep. I reluctantly agreed and got the nurse to help him as I made my way back to the hotel, lost in my thoughts.

I decided to walk instead of taking the late bus so I could clear my head and think about what this meant for Dad and for me. It all seemed so real. When we prayed, it finally went away. I asked God to stay watching over him so that the vulture would not return.

When I got to the hotel I fell on my bed exhausted. I ended up sleeping with the lights on for several hours, because every time I turned them off, I could see dad's demon. I was up and on my way back to Dad by sunrise on Sunday morning.

I wanted to be by his side and to make sure that there were no more unwanted visitors. I was hoping my presence would make a difference.

I know how
Just quite how
My life and love might still go on
In your heart
In your mind
I'll stay with you for all of time

-Lyrics from "Wherever You Will Go"
by The Calling

CHAPTER 23

I got to the hospital very early. Dad was still sleeping. I didn't even bring coffee or breakfast for him. I just wanted to get there and be with him because I knew we were running out of time. I also wanted to make sure there were no more unwanted visitors. Breakfast could wait for a few hours. I would go out and get him whatever he wanted when he was ready.

"I've had a good life," he said out of nowhere.

I perked up right away. I didn't even realize he was awake yet.

As I rubbed my eyes I replied, "Yeah you have dad, but don't start talking like that. You will probably out-live us all", I said in an effort to lighten the mood.

He looked at me with a hint of sarcasm, raising an eyebrow in my direction. I suddenly felt ashamed by my feeble attempt. I brushed it off, pulled my chair up closer to him and sat silently waiting for him to speak. I could tell he wanted to talk, and I really wanted to hear what he had to say.

I will never forget.

"Michael, I have lived a good, long life. And if my time is now, I am ready to go with no regrets and with a full heart. I had a great profession for forty-five years. I had an amazing life with my family and the feelings I have for all of you will always be. I have lived and loved a lifetime. I can tell you one thing that I know for certain, from a seventy-six year old fart.

As a smile broke across my face I silently thought to myself, this is our "Tuesdays with Morrie" moment, dad-style!

"I know now that there is nothing more important in life than love. Love and the unforgettable, breathtaking moments that love brings are what we live for and what matters the most. Everything else is just noise."

Who and what we love makes us who we are and the moments, the special, unforgettable moments that we get to experience as we share and cultivate that love is what makes life worth living. I am certain of this.

Life is not always easy. You know? We make mistakes, deal with pain and sometimes tragedy. Some-times life knocks us down. You know what I did when life knocked me down? I got back up. All of you kids, you, Janet, Rich and Danny. You all need to get back up when life knocks you down. You gotta get back up and keep pushing to find what you love and embrace the moments it brings.

It doesn't matter how much money you make or how much stuff you accumulate in your life. It doesn't matter where you live or what your social status is, your title or list of accolades. It means nothing if you don't love. It means nothing if you aren't loved.

None of the bullshit that we make important outside of this matters, because I'm telling your right now pee-wee, you can't take any of it with you.

The only thing that you can take with you, the only thing that survives beyond our lives is love and the love that you leave behind for others to remember you by."

I just sat there, staring at him, savoring this moment. I was in awe. He seemed to have a lightness to him, almost like a new energy emanating from him that hadn't been there before.

I found myself thinking about what he was saying and

thinking about my experiences over the last ten days. There was a certain type of synergy between what I had been feeling, what I had been searching for, what I now felt and what he was saying. It was all colliding into the same space but I didn't know how to pull it all together or how to make it all make sense.

As I was lost in my thoughts, he finally looked over at me and said, "how about some breakfast?" He was hungry again. Perfect!

"You got it!" I said as I sprung to my feet. "What'll it be?"

He chose eggs and sausage with hash browns and black coffee. I could hardly believe it!

I shuffled out of the ICU and down the street with an extra spring in my step. It would take me a while to digest everything he just said and to apply it to my life. I couldn't help thinking how proud I was of him and how proud I was to be his son. This was a great moment.

CHAPTER 24

Less than twenty four hours until the arrival of the air ambulance, I was dozing off in my usual place at Dad's side. It was around seven in the afternoon and the sun was just starting to set. The ICU was quiet and all that could be heard was the hum of the various machines spread throughout the room. I had grown so used to it, in fact I was actually comfortable. In reality, I think I was riding the high of my last conversation with Dad and the fact that I was about to set him on his way home.

The end of my marathon was only one day away and one cross planet flight from being over. After all he had been through and all I had done to secure his trip home, I was certain now that he would make it. I continued to pray for his safety and his soul. It wasn't like I was taught to pray as a child. Even as an adult, I had always just said the words and never really felt them. But ever since the incident with the vulture lady, the words to the prayers meant more. Now when I said "Deliver us from evil", I really meant it. I kept saying it over and over as I continued my one way dialog with God.

Out of the corner of my eye I noticed Dad was looking up again. "Oh no!" I thought. But as I studied his face, I could see that this time something was different. This time his face didn't show any of the fear of the vulture lady.

This time, his face had a sense of peace. There was wonder and awe in his eyes. It was as if he was seeing someone familiar and welcoming. I immediately knew something very different and very special was going on. In the back of my mind, I thought of Pop Pop and his visions. A wave of emotions came over me as I thought to myself, "This is real. Pop Pop's visions were real and now Dad is having them too."

"Dad? Who is it?"

A few seconds of peaceful silence passed by as I wiped the corners of my suddenly filled eyes.

"She's beautiful. Just beautiful."

"Who is it, Dad? What does she look like?"

"Oh my! He said breathlessly. Wow! This is in-credible!"

"She is smiling at me. She has long flowing dark hair and a long flowing white dress. There is a blue sash around her waist, with a blue ribbon tied in her hair. She looks so calm and happy. There is a light shining around her that is filling the room. She has her arms spread out like she wants to hug me. She is talking to me but I can't hear her yet."

My God, I thought! Is this really happening? Is this real? Did he just say "Yet?"

I didn't even consider asking him what he meant by "yet." In my heart, I knew. I felt the same presence that I felt on the mountain in the rain. It was here for Dad. It was completely and utterly overwhelming.

I felt a wave of peace and satisfaction engulf me. I knew it was almost time and that I had done what I came here to do. My eyes were filled with tears of love, a single drop rolled down my cheek. I felt a tremendous sense of love and compassion for Dad. I felt a little envious as I watched him study her.

I knew that he was soon going to be in better hands and a better place. Pop Pop saw the visions three days before he died and now Dad was seeing them too. I had no doubts left anymore. Every inch of my skin stood on edge as a feeling of contentment filled my body, mind and soul. I quietly moved back to my lawn chair and sunk in as dad continued to look in to the heavens. I just sat and watched him. I didn't want to disturb this moment and this connection he was having. I silently prayed a thanks to God for this amazing experience and for looking after Dad.

I had seen and felt too much in the last ten days to continue to blindly label all that had happened as chance or ghost stories. I had no doubts anymore, I believed. With conviction, I finally believed and found what had been eluding me my entire life. I found faith, where I least expected it.

Something great and something special was happening to Dad and I was witness to it. I wonder if I will get to see what he saw before I die. I hope so. I can do without the vulture lady, though.

The rest of the night was peaceful and quiet. We both reflected on the events of the past few days. Dad continued to talk about how much he was looking forward to going home. I didn't interrupt him or offer any alternatives. I wanted him to believe that his life would get back to normal. He would need to believe that in order to make it home.

I realized that it was a gift to be here with him for what I knew were his final days. I was thankful that he was himself right up until the very end. After he had seen the Angel, a peace had come over Dad and I wondered if he knew what it meant. I thought about bringing up Pop Pop's visions but decided against it. His vitals improved a little and he had an air of confidence about him. It was as if he wasn't afraid anymore. Previously, I could detect his fear and a hesitation, but it was gone now.

I stayed in that lawn chair next to Dad for the entire night. I didn't want to leave his side. Dad slept calmly and peacefully, he was clearly at peace. I restlessly fell in and out of sleep. I thought briefly about opening my laptop, but work was not an option for me tonight. I couldn't think about anything other than the experience of the last ten days. They all played through my mind on repeat. I spent most of the night reflecting on the implications of it all.

As the sun started coming up, I began what I knew would be the last day I would ever see my Dad.

CHAPTER 25

So this was it and I knew it. After a nice day together filled a few naps and a lot of idle conversation, it was finally time. It was approaching seven pm and I was sitting in the hall, waiting to go back in. I was numb and exhausted but somehow, I had done it. The Lear jet was here to take Dad home.

I was scared to say goodbye. My heart was beating against my chest so hard that it felt like a jackhammer. Forty years of life together came down to this moment. Forty years of a father's unwavering love and devotion for his son. Forty years of a son's unconditional love and emotional surrender to his father.

A final goodbye. A final embrace.

I wasn't ready. I just knew that this would be the last time I would ever see him and I wasn't ready for it. I was falling apart inside.

I had no idea what I wanted to say and I had no idea if he knew that this was the last time he would see me. My emotions were swelling inside me like a tsunami ready to break against the walls of a dam.

It had been 10 days since this journey began and I was as physically and emotionally strung out as a person could be. I had held it together through the trip, through caring for him, through the logistical nightmare of arranging his air ambulance, through the pain of his dark visions. I had been running a physical and emotional marathon for weeks and I hadn't had a second to prepare for this moment.

I was torn between wanting to say goodbye to him and wanting to say the right thing. I did not want to scare him or tell him what I knew of his fate. After the last vision he had, I thought he must know. But it seemed as though he was still hanging on to the hope and illusion that once he got home he would recover. As irrational as it was, I was thankful for it because it delayed his fears and gave him some peace.

The door opened slowly and Dr. Klein stuck her head out and gave me a nod and smile. It was time.

I don't remember smiling back at her or walking in or even breathing. The medical team was at the foot of the bed in a semi-circle. They had finished preparing their trays and set his new IV's. They were going to sedate and intubate him the minute I gave the go ahead, but for now he was completely lucid. He was exhausted and battered, but his final thoughts were as sharp as he was in every phase of my life. After all he had been through, I thought that was amazing. I was proud of him.

The airplane was in the hangar, refueled and ready to go. The air ambulance team was outside making their final checklists.

Dad began to speak softly. He looked at the medical team with a look of peace and pure gratitude.

"I ... I have no words. There are no words," he said to the team.

He choked down the last part. There was no language barrier or translation necessary this time. He knew he had died twice and they brought him back. He hadn't been ready. I wondered if he was now. There was a moment of complete silence. I could hear my own heart beating.

Then quietly, Dr. Klein walked to him, bent down and stroked the side of his face. He looked into her eyes and simply said, "Thank you" with as much gratitude as a person could express. She gave him a warm, compassionate smile and in broken English said, "You are very welcome. Good luck to you Michael. God bless you." And she kissed him on the forehead for a long second and then slowly backed away.

She straightened and looked to me, giving me a nod that meant it was my turn. She turned her back to us in an attempt to give us some privacy. The rest of the crew took her cue and turned away. I knew this was the last moment I would ever see him. But I still didn't know what to say. I lost my words. I lost my ability to speak.

I stepped to the side of the bed. Tears were forming in my eyes but I had to try to be strong for him. I didn't want to make him scared. I swallowed hard and pursed my lips to keep it inside. Quietly and without a word he reached his hand up extending it towards mine. I grabbed it, locking our thumbs together in a strong embrace. He still felt strong to me, even now. I stared into his eyes as the tears started to flow down my face. He looked back at me with a look of strength, gratitude and a sense that he knew. He had a peace about him that was very calming to me.

I tried to speak but no words would come. I was choking back the emotion. There was so much I wanted desperately to say. There was so much to thank him for, and even at my age...so much to ask him for. No matter how hard I tried, no words would come. I just kept looking at him, trying to speak, trying to say everything I needed to say but I couldn't.

A smile broke across his face and he said, "Hey. I know. I know. OK? It's OK. You did good! You did good, Michael. Thank You he said as he squeezed my hand in a strong embrace."

I couldn't believe it. Once again, one final time, he was the strong one. I was forty years old and still in desperate need of my dad's approval and he knew it and was willing to give it to me. It felt good.

I was able to let out a broken, "I love you, dad" as I leaned down and buried my head to his shoulder. Just as I had done when I was five and was scared after my trauma, just as I had done on the football field that day in Hershey, just as I had done when Mom died. It was one of the defining moments of my life and one that will never leave me.

I stood up as tears streamed down my cheeks. The doctors moved in. I said one last goodbye and started to leave the room. There were no poignant speeches, no words of great wisdom, no drama. Instead, as I backed toward the door, keeping my eyes on him the entire time, he looked up extended his hand, and gave me the finger point. One last time. It was perfect.

I couldn't talk anymore so I just gave him the chest thump back three times as I caught myself from falling apart.

The finger point is the last and most appropriate image of my Dad that I have and one I cherish and think about often. Dr. Klein moved back to his side and with her broken English said, "Are you ready, Michael?" He kept his eyes locked with mine as he replied, "Yes. I'm ready."

I knew he was ready. I knew this was it. I knew I would never see him again.

As the door closed and a flurry of activity began behind it, I slowly stepped out into the hall, walked down to the bench at the end of it and sat down to collect myself. It was dark. It was getting late, the sun had just set. Visiting hours were over. I was alone. I was really all alone now. In a state of exhaustion, triumph and relief, the waves of emotion that I was building up, finally took me. I put my head into my hands and my elbows on my knees and began quietly sobbing

CHAPTER 26

It seemed like I sat in that dark hallway forever. It must have been only a few minutes in reality but I couldn't tell the difference. It felt like time had stopped and I couldn't move. It was as if I was watching someone else live these moments and I could only stand by, motionless and drained. I couldn't affect it or even communicate anymore. Thoughts were swirling of the events of the last ten days. I was relieved to know that I did everything possible to get him home and to let his life end with dignity, the way he wanted.

After some silent reflection, I finally began pulling myself together. I slowly got up and started making my way out of the hospital. I had to stop in the bathroom to clean myself up. I looked in the mirror, and I couldn't even recognize myself. My eyes were red, my shirt was spotted with tears. My hair was disheveled, my knee was sore and my shin splints were on fire. My entire body ached. In short, I was a mess. I hadn't slept well for the last ten days. I don't know what was worse, the physical or the emotional exhaustion. I was on empty. I had nothing left to give.

I couldn't stop wondering what would happen to him now. I continued to grapple with what I had seen, felt and experienced while I was here and how real it was. I had a strong knowing that the angel was there with him to guide him and that was comforting.

I didn't stay to watch them wheel dad out. I didn't want my last image of him to be unconscious with a tube in his mouth. I knew he was in good hands and I just knew that he would make it home. I wanted our last embrace to be my last memory of him. I wanted the finger point to be the lasting image in my mind. That was my dad. Strength above all and love for his family.

As I began my journey back to the hotel to pack for my flight to Denver in the morning, I felt a peace come over me. My mission here was complete. It felt good to finally know that that there was something else out there. Something beautiful and loving, welcoming and all encompassing. I don't know exactly what it was that Dad experienced, but I know this. It was real. And I truly believe it is out there waiting for all of us.

CHAPTER 27

Dad's journey back to Harrisburg began before my journey back to Boulder, but was going to exceed mine by almost a day. By the time he made it home, I would have already be home for a night. His journey would be close to 30 hours. Of course he would be unconscious the entire time. I was still hoping and praying that his heart would hold out the whole way. I couldn't imagine that after everything we had been through over the last ten days and after all that he had survived in the last month that he could die now before he made it home. He just needed to hold on a little longer.

As I boarded the night train from Salzburg to Munich, Dad embarked on the first leg of his private flight from Salzburg to Reykjavik, Iceland. The plane took off around ten o'clock at night. The Lear jet would land in Iceland around five o'clock in the morning. They would spend the morning there, never leaving the plane. After performing their safety checks and refueling, they would take off in the morning a few hours after the Lufthansa Airbus I was on took off from Munich.

By the time I was landing in Denver, Dad would have completed the second leg of his flight from Iceland to Greenland. It was too bad he couldn't be awake to get out of the plane and enjoy such a beautiful place. They were not able to send us updates, so we all just waited and speculated about where they might be. This was before flight tracking was as prevalent as it is today. They would arrive in Greenland late in the morning, refuel, perform their maintenance and plot their course for the next stop. All the while, they maintained Dad's vitals as best they could.

His ejection fraction was dangerously low, which was a signal that his heart could barely pump any longer. They kept him under anesthesia the entire way without any major issues. He was holding on but he wasn't even halfway there yet.

The leg from Greenland to Canada would be the longest, as it crossed the Atlantic. All I could picture was his still body being kept alive by machines, holding on against all odds as he crossed the globe.

Meanwhile, my flight home was very uneventful. I spent the eleven hour flight fading in and out of a restless sleep, writing more of Dad's eulogy and contemplating all that I had experienced. I felt a warm-ness and a peace spread throughout my body as I reflected. It was a feeling I have searched for and craved ever since.

I had already landed in Denver before Dad even got to Canada. He was several hours behind me, or so I figured. They would refuel and do extended safety checks before heading out for Detroit, the last stop before getting to Harrisburg.

After that, it would be a short flight to Harrisburg where an ambulance would be waiting to take him to the Community General Osteopathic Hospital. Danny and Rich would be waiting there for him and I am sure they would not leave his side for anything once he arrived. This happened to be the same hospital where Mom died, which was fitting.

I could suddenly picture Mom in her temporary apartment anxiously waiting for Dad to get there so she could show him around the place. Dad would be so happy to see Max again, too. The thought made me smile.

As I was beginning my morning, the jet should have landed in Harrisburg. However when I checked my phone to see if anyone had checked in. There was nothing.

CHAPTER 28

It had been a restless night but I was able to get some sleep thanks to my extreme exhaustion. It was good to be home with my kids and I was pleased to be slowly start getting back into the routine of things.

I had gotten up early to take Ethan to his hockey camp. I decided I would take him to keep my mind occupied. Megan was helpful and compassionate even though we both knew that things were definitely never going to be same. It was weighing on me heavily but after what I had been through, I was not ready to face it and Megan understood that. She was kind and supportive and I was thankful for that.

While I was making my way to the YMCA for the clinic, Dad's plane had finally landed in Harrisburg, his journey almost complete. Within minutes he was transported from the airplane to the ambulance and promptly rushed from the Harrisburg International Airport.

After more than thirty hours of travel the ambulance finally pulled up to the emergency room entrance at the Osteopathic Hospital. Danny and Rich were there at the emergency entrance waiting for him. They went through hell waiting for him to get home, dropped everything in their lives and rushed to be by his side. Rich had driven all through the night from Michigan and hadn't slept in two days. Rich would have done anything for Dad. Danny had switched shifts with another cop to be there. I was so grateful that they were there for Dad.

Rich and Danny walked alongside Dad's gurney as they wheeled him through the same labyrinth of hallways that I traversed to be there for Mom years ago. As they walked they studied Dad's stitches and scars, his sunken eyes and his pale skin. It was an emotional moment for both of them. Rich had to temporarily look away in order to hold himself together.

They rounded the final corner in the seemingly endless labyrinth, and finally arrived at Dad's private room in the ICU. They situated Dad's bed and connected his monitoring devices and IVs. They gave him some medicine that would start to bring him out of his drug induced state. Danny and Rich both stood on each side of his bed and spoke to him. "Dad, we're here. You're home. We got you home. You're home now. Don't worry about anything else. Michael got you home. We won't leave your side. OK? You are here with us now," they kept repeating.

Amazingly, in what seemed like a matter of a few short minutes, Dad began to open his eyes. He blinked as he tried to gain his bearings and take in his surroundings. He was trying to focus and seemed to slowly become more aware of where he was and who was with him. He looked from Danny to Rich, and then did a double take.

In that instant it was clear, he knew he was home. His eyes lit up with relief and excitement. His sons were here with him. Rich and Danny continued to tell him how great it was to see him. As they spoke, their eyes filled with tears of love and compassion that spilled down their cheeks.

Dad was able to reach both of his hands towards Rich and Danny's. They quickly embraced the hand that was offered. Dad gave each of their hands a weakened squeeze and nodding as he looked toward the heavens. A single tear pooled and escaped down his cheek as he took one last look at his sons. He was where he wanted to be. He laid his head back, and closed his eyes for the last time as his hands slowly lost their grip and fell idle.

The medical staff came rushing in as they saw his heart monitor go flat. Rich stopped them as they approached the bed and choked out as best as he could, "No, please...let him go...let him be. No heroic measures. It's done."

And so on August 5, 2009, at approximately 2:17 PM, my Dad died.

He died where he wanted, when he wanted and with whom he wanted. He fought to get here. He fought through two heart failures, a twice-busted head, a bad back and a trip across the world.

I was sitting in the YMCA watching my son go through his hockey drills, when I felt my phone buzz. I knew right away who and what it was. Looking down at the caller ID and seeing Danny's number was only a further confirmation.

I answered my phone and calmly said "Hey"

Danny responded quietly "Michael, he's gone."

I had a moment of pause and reflection with my brother. I told him how thankful I was that he and Rich had been there and we said our goodbyes.

No one could possibly know what the last ten days together with Dad were like and no one could possibly understand all of the things I experienced with him.

I know now that I was a spiritual utensil which was being utilized by something far beyond my comprehension. I was able to connect to something that I always wanted to believe was real. Now I knew, it was all real and that Dad's consciousness or soul was somewhere else right now, intact. I was certain.

I was overwhelmed with satisfaction and peace, the ordeal was over. I remember thinking that nothing could ever possibly be the same for me.

"I'm alive.
Even though a part of me has died.
You take this heart and breathe it
Back to life.
I fall into your arms open wide.
When the hurt and the healer collide."

-Lyrics from Hurt and the Healer by Mercy Me

CHAPTER 29

Six days later, I sat in the pew of our family church in Harrisburg, half listening to the scripture and the rituals of a traditional Catholic funeral. My attention was focused on the eulogy I was about to deliver. I had been up for most of the night finishing it. In fact, I had been writing it on and off from the time I got on the flight to Germany.

I felt a sense of spiritual responsibility to ensure that his eulogy was properly delivered and received. In my mind I knew he would be standing there listening to me. I pictured him pacing back and forth in front of his cascade with his arms folded like he had always done, fingers pinched by his mouth as he listened intently. I wrote it so he could be proud of the life he lived as he heard me talk about him. These are the kind of words that I wish I could have spoken to him before he died. But I had no doubt he would hear them now.

It was a brutally hot August day. The air conditioning was on full force in the church as mourners began pouring in. I was disappointed that his funeral had to be during the week on a Thursday morning at ten. I was worried that not a lot of people would be able to come due to their work schedules and other commitments. Saturday morning would have been more appropriate, but the church was already booked so we settled for a Thursday. My fears were soon allayed as the church began filling up with mourners, friends, colleagues and well-wishers.

Prior to the mourners being let in the church, they unlocked Dad's casket and let the family have one last goodbye. Ethan and Christian drew goodbye cards to him in crayon, saying goodbye to their "Gampy" in their own way. We filled his casket with the cards from the kids, a copy of his eulogy, a Pittsburgh Steelers hat, a stethoscope, a beer and a picture of the entire family. Once we filled all of the items we each had our final moment with him. As I took mine, I looked down and took a quick second to scan his face. I had already had my goodbye with him a week earlier and as I gazed down upon his body I knew that it wasn't dad anymore. This was a vessel that held my Dad for seventy-six years but it wasn't him. They didn't even prepare his hair the way he wore it, they had it slicked straight back. I am sure he would have wanted it combed to right. I reached down and fixed his hair, pushing it to the side and fixing the part. I turned away and never looked back.

The service was a typical Catholic mass with the priest talking about death not being the end but another beginning. I had heard this many times in my life, but for the first time in my life I was sure it was true.

After communion was over, it was almost my turn. My palms were sweating and my heart was throbbing in my chest. I was emotional and I wanted to make sure I did justice to his life and I hoped he would be happy with what I wrote.

After several moments of silent prayer and reflection the priest moved out to the front of the altar and introduced me. "And now, to read Michael's eulogy is his youngest son, Michael Peterson, Jr.

You could hear a pin drop. No one was moving. Not a sound.

My journey that led me from across the world, up a mountain top and brought me face to face with a demon, was about to culminate on that podium. I was about to step up and let everyone know who he was and what he meant to me.

I don't remember walking out of the pew and to the podium. I don't remember seeing anyone. I don't re-member breathing. All eyes were on me and I felt the collective compassion in the church. It was calming.

In that moment, I felt clarity. My heart stopped pounding and I felt ready to say everything that I was not able to say. I had a sense of calm and purpose and confidence come over me as I took a deep breath and began.

I would like to welcome and thank you for coming to honor and celebrate the life of my Dad, Dr. Michael Peterson. Today we reflect on the legacy he left behind on August 5, 2007.

It is not possible to summarize my Dad's life and the legacy he left behind in a 10 minute eulogy. Where do you start? How can you possibly explain the depths of his life and his soul and its impact on all of us? It is not possible. The proper words really don't exist.

So I am not going to even try. Instead, I would like to share some details of his life that everyone here and many that are not here, in some way, had the privilege to share in. I'd like to tell you a little bit about my Dad.

After he died, I learned that he was known to many people over the years in many different capacities and had many different titles or nicknames throughout his life;

Some people called him Mickey.

To some he was Doc, Doc Pete or Doctor Peterson.

To some he was Coach.

To some he was Teacher.

To some he was Colleague and Mentor.

To one, he was a Husband.

To all, he was a Friend.

And for four of us who were lucky enough, we got to call him Dad.

To anyone who knew him, you knew that he was

real and human, flawed and gifted, talented and a regular guy; inside and out, all at once.

To say he was selfless and unassuming would be to understate the character upon which he built his life, family, career and his legacy.

He was brilliant, thoughtful and introspective. He was eloquent and precise. He was humorous and hard working.

He was sure of himself and who he was with a kind of absolute clarity that defined him as a man and endeared him to so many.

He had a heart the size of a mountain and a boot the size of Pittsburgh and he wasn't afraid of using either.

He was ambitious but not in a way that was for his own gain. His was a purpose that was not based in self. His ambition was as a physician, husband and father – and he did all with equal imperfect perfection. He wasn't perfect. None of us are. But his intentions and values for his family guided him and set him on his life's course. And he never lost sight of that, even until his final days.

Dad's legacy lives on in everyone that he touched through the course of his life. His is a legacy of unconditional love, self-sacrifice, determination, passion, fortitude and family.

He was born on September 18, 1930 in a tiny coal mining town in upstate Pennsylvania called Glenn Lyon. To say it was a small town would be an understatement. The population of the entire town was less than 2000.

His father John, began his life's work as a coal miner at the young age of 14, forced into hard labor to support his family after his father died. He worked in the coal mines for over 40 years until finally, the mine was shut down. His mother, Anna raised the family of 5 children. When the mines shut down, Anna went to work in the local sewing factory to keep food on the table.

They were extremely poor but the children never knew it. There were no elaborate vacations, no luxuries and no material fascinations. There was hard work and there was family.

Dad used to say that his family was from the "old country," and they were. In every sense of the word they were "old school". From his family, Dad inherited toughness, an incomparable work ethic and a resilience that defined him and set the foundation for the person he was to become.

He was particularly close with his sister Angela, who is here today. Angela and dad were only 16 months apart and were best friends. They did everything together. They played together, laughed together, shared a paper route together, sometimes fought together, and stayed close until his last days.

As Dad was nearing the end of his life, Angela was rushing to the hospital in Harrisburg to be at his side and to tell him that it was OK for him to let go. Unfortunately, Dad passed away before she got there. Angela, you may not have made it in time to say the words – but please let me assure you, He knew. He knew how much you loved him. He loved you dearly and unconditionally and he took that with him. In his last days, lying in his hospital bed in Salzburg, Austria, his eyes growing dark, his thoughts were of you. He wanted to make sure that you were informed of his condition and that you were OK.

I had to pause and swallow down my emotion. I took a long, deep breath and began again.

After high school, Dad decided to join the

Marines and went to enlist with his cousin, Terry. As fate would have it, Dad failed the entry physical because he had a ruptured ear drum. As a result, the marines did not accept him, although they did accept Terry.

Shortly after, Terry was sent to Korea where he was killed in battle by a mortar shell that landed only feet from where he was patrolling.

Dad did not take the rejection from the Marines well and vowed to serve his country in spite of his ear drum. Later that year, he was accepted into the Air Force and was stationed in Germany for a three year term. This strange twist of fate, masked in the form of a broken ear drum, is one of the key defining points of his life. To think about all of the lives that were affected by that one tiny ear drum is to believe in divine intervention and destiny.

In Germany, Dad was assigned to be a medic. It awoke something inside of him. He dis-covered an untapped passion. It was during these years in the service as a young man that he found himself and what he was to become. He was so enthralled with medicine that when his tour of duty was up, he re-enlisted for another three year term. This is when he knew he was to be a doctor.

After his second tour of duty finished, he was honorably discharged from the Air Force. He then began his undergraduate studies at the University of Scranton. He was able to fund his college through student loans and by working full time as there was no money available to pay his tuition. During his schooling, he worked in a funeral home, transporting the dead and preparing them for their funerals. For the four years of his undergraduate schooling, he lived in the up-stairs room at the funeral home. Clearly, this was one determined man. He graduated with honors from Scranton and set his sights on *medical school.*

In those years, medical school was not an option open to just anyone. Connections were vital and he had none. He was met with rejections from many institutions but he persevered – he would not accept failure – finally, after years of trying, he ended up getting a fellowship to the University of Tennessee medical school at Memphis.

He did not begin medical school until he was thirty-two years old. Most people by that time believe that medical school is too daunting to take on, but not Dad. He knew who he was and who he wanted to be. He worked hard to achieve his dream.

And so at age 36, in 1966, he graduated from the University of Tennessee Medical school. He did it. He set his dream, went after it and achieved it.

Dad met his wife Janice Denton, our mom, at the University of Scranton. They got to know each other over time by doing their laundry together. They became inseparable and fell in love, getting married in 1958, spending more than 46 years of marriage together and raising a family of 4 of their own.

Mom passed away in 2004. We all find comfort in knowing that she was there waiting for him and that they are together again.

Dad had a calling to use his unique abilities to help people through the practice of medicine. It was what he loved, and who he was. He was able to positively affect so many people's lives due to his unparalleled passion and fortitude.

Mom and Dad moved to Harrisburg, Pennsylvania in 1966 as Dad did his medical residency at Polyclinic Medical Center, commencing on a 40 year journey of family, friends and his medical practice.

To those of you that were his patients – on behalf of our Dad, I want to say thank you. You touched him in ways that you will never know. He loved being a doctor. It truly is what he was born to do. He loved making a difference in all of your lives. And most of all, he loved just being a part of your lives.

We remember growing up – it didn't matter where we were. The mall. A movie. A picnic. A football game, the park, or out at a restaurant.

There were always a smiling face and a "Hey Doc" to greet us everywhere we went. And he always knew your names. Always. We remember when we were young, not fully understanding what Dad did for a living and thinking "Wow, my Dad must be really important." And he was. But as important as he was in your lives – you were more important to his. You should know this.

I remember watching him hop a fence and climb over bleachers at a football game to assist a man who was dying from a heart attack – we all watched, gasping in silence as Dad per-formed heroic measures and revived him – saving his life.

Again, I remember thinking as a very young boy, "who in the world is this guy?" and knowing in the heart of a child that my Dad was my hero. I wanted to be just like him. I still do.

This is just one of many examples of great acts that he performed during his practicing years.

Growing up, we had to share him with all of you – but we always knew, even as children, how important his work was and how important he was in the lives of his patients. We remember the midnight phone calls, house calls, emergencies, stress, the tireless hours, the heartache when he would lose someone, the elation when he would save someone – through it all, He loved it. It was who he was destined to be.

Many years later, he relayed a story to us that illustrates what it all meant to him. He was seventy five years old and still practicing medicine, although the business of medicine had grown thin on him over the years. You see, he was "old school" in every sense of the word. He would rather look you in the eye and tell you what was wrong and how to fix it – or if it couldn't be fixed, to lend you a strong shoulder to the end. He wasn't very interested in lawyers or liabilities or the pressures of modern day medicine that had nothing to do with caring for his patients.

As news of his pending retirement began to make its way through town, an elderly couple that had been coming to see him for more than 30 years came into the office because they had heard. They heard he would be retiring and they just wanted to come by to say "Thanks, Doc. Thank you for taking care of our family for all of those years." When he heard this, he broke down. When he told the story to us later, he broke down and wept again. He wept because it was time for him to let go of what drove him for all of those years. He had to let go of all of you.

Shortly after his retirement, Dad was proudly displaying a greeting card that he had received in the mail on his kitchen table. In the card was a heartfelt message from a woman who had learned of Dad's retirement. He shared the card with tremendous pride, satisfaction and a lump in his throat.

The card was from a woman whose daughter was afflicted with cancer at a very young age. It spoke of how grateful the family was to Dad for his quick diagnosis, his quick action, his directness in telling them their options and chances --- and for his broad shoulders when times got the hardest. Her card spoke of how her family found strength from

Dad that they did not have in themselves. When they didn't feel like they could face the next day's events, Dad was there. They appreciated his style, his steadiness, his compassion and his vigilance.

Thankfully, that little girl grew up and is still with us today. When he finished reading the letter, he had tears streaming down his cheeks as he sat in his chair, his hands wiping the tears as he said, "That is why I did it. That is what it's all about." To the woman who sent that card, if you are here today, thank you. You touched him more than you can possibly know.

I paused again, telling myself to keep it together. I had to make it through this.

It is with heavy hearts that we are here today to say goodbye to someone who was everything to us – our provider, our guide, our support when times got tough, our pride when we felt life's triumphs, our conscience when we strayed from our path, and our rock when we didn't think we could get back up from a fall.

We know that Dad is here today and listening. There are times when we think to ourselves, "What am I going to do without you?"

But when we feel lost and like we can't overcome our struggles, we need to look no further than the legacy that you left for us through the details of your life. We can look at the obstacles you overcame, how you lived your life and how you loved us through it all. We will still find our strength in you and in the examples you set for us all.

I had the privilege and gift of being with Dad in the final days of his life. From his hospital bed in Salzburg, Austria, I will never forget what he told me and I will do my best to live that way and to pass on to my kids and even to all of you. When he knew his time had come, he became reflective on his life and life in general and he told me, "Find what you love. Seek it. Don't stop until you find it. And once you find it, cherish it. Protect it and defend it. In the end, love is the only thing that matters and it is the only thing you can take with you."

Dad, I know you are listening. I promise you, I will persevere to find what I love fiercely, give it all I've got and never give up. And then I will pass it on, as if it were a torch, to those who follow me. This is what I learned from you. This is your legacy and it will always live on.

I looked up and could see many people wiping tears from their eyes. Some were looking at me and nodding their head in approval, some were smiling with an expression of compassion and understanding.

That was my Dad. And I love him more than I could possibly express into words. Until we see each other again ...

At that point, I did the finger point up to the sky. Up to Dad.

(end)

CHAPTER 30

The evening after the funeral, I was numb, exhausted and becoming more and more reflective on the journey I had just completed. I kept replaying in my mind the feeling I had that night on the mountain and how real it was. I couldn't get over the experiences of what Dad saw and I was still struggling to figure out what it all meant. I found that once I stopped questioning them and I let them sink in, it was comforting. I felt a peace that was previously foreign to me.

It was a source of peace to think, even for a second, that Mom and Dad were out there somewhere. That they still existed. That they were OK and safe and that I would see them again. But at the same time, I still had that other voice in my head telling me that it was all hooey and a figment of my imagination. My mind and my spirit were now in a tug of war over what to believe. But I was clear on what I wanted to believe and what I desperately wanted to be true.

It was past dusk now and as the darkness of night descended on Harrisburg, I was heading to Dad's house for what would be the last time. I had to make one last sweep through the house for my things and in truth, I wanted to have a quiet moment there on my own as a sort of a final goodbye.

Everyone had already gone their separate ways in an unceremonious fashion. Janet went back to Richmond, Danny went back to Lancaster and Rich began his journey back to Michigan. We had a final short embrace with each other, each of us expressing our sadness in our own way.

Now that Dad was gone, things would never be the same. But it was time to get back to our own lives and problems. For me, it was time to deal with the inevitability of my marriage ending and figure out how to make it as easy as possible on the kids. I felt a heavy weight; as if I wasn't ready to leave yet and that I hadn't done all that I came here to do. My feelings of doubt over my faith were forefront in my mind.

The four of us had already agreed to sell the house as soon as we could but it was not without some hesitation on my part. There were generations full of memories in that house that had been accumulated over the last forty years. Danny agreed to take charge of the cleaning out of the house, the division of salvageable things and ultimately the sale of the home that we all grew up in together. It was a sobering, cold, empty feeling that it was all over. Now it was just a bunch of walls, floors and space. It was no longer our home.

I was very appreciative that Danny was willing to handle the house on his own. He would consult with us on important things like the sell price, timing and to evaluate the offers we would receive. I felt that I had more than done my part by going to Salzburg and getting Dad home. He knew he had an enormous amount of work ahead of him, but Danny never complained and just did what had to be done.

As I was driving through the old, familiar streets of Harrisburg where I spent my childhood and early adult years, I started feeling intense emotion about going to the house for the last time. This would be the last trip home that I would ever take. Now that Mom and Dad were gone, it wasn't even home anymore and I had no desire to go back after this one last goodbye. Our Mom and Dad were what made that house our home. In that space was all of our memories. Some of the memories were good. Some of the memories were bad. We had more than our share of triumphs, and even a few tragedies. But all in all, this house was the anchor point, the safe port in the face of any tempest we found ourselves in throughout our lives. This is the house where I was taken home as a baby, where I grew up, where we laughed, where we cried, where Mom and Dad raised us into the men and woman we had become.

Of course, with any family, there is good and bad. There are times throughout the last forty years when we were not great to each other. We all carry around scars with us from things that hurt us over the years or from things that we would rather forget. But after this experience I realize that none of that matters anymore. It really doesn't. It is not important. Hanging on to pain and anger only compromises our lives and creates an anchor of negativity that gets in the way of our ability to live our lives to the fullest. I choose to remember the good. Now that they were both gone, it didn't seem to make much sense to focus on anything other than the best memories of my life with them.

The sun had already set and the familiar clear, dark central Pennsylvania night time sky was all around. The blue asphalt of the streets was offset by the bright highlighter yellow of the lines in the center of each road. The trees were in full bloom and swaying in the light breeze, giving off the slightest scent of honeysuckle. My senses were alive and I was taking in every sight, sound and smell of this old, familiar place. It still felt like home.

I pulled up to the stop sign at the top of Hastey Drive and stayed there for a long while. I was completely unaware of everything else around me. I tuned out the radio. There was no other traffic which made the neighborhood feel deserted. I felt alone. As I looked down to the end of the street, I imagined seeing Dad in the distance giving me the finger point just like he had done for all those years. It made me smile. It meant so much to me and even more so now. After a while, I finally made the left turn onto Hastey Dr. for the last time.

I crept down the street, making sure to take in every aspect of the place. The woods that lined the back of the houses along the west side of Hastey Drive seemed untouched, dark and still.

The car slowly rolled by the sidewalks where I ran as a teenager, the same sidewalks we road our bikes and skateboards down as kids. I remembered all of the games we used to play, the snowmen we built, the forts we constructed for our snowball fights and all of the friends we had over the years. I recalled the birthday parties, the holiday decorations, going trick or treating every year, and walking the dog.

Rich, Danny and I used to change the blade height on the lawn mower and mow a nine-hole golf course into the grass around the house. We would use plastic golf balls and wrap them in hockey tape so they flew further. We took exceptional care to cut the greens lower than the fare ways and to leave the weeds as high as possible. We even created an island in the weeds just like the 17th hole at Augusta. Those were great times together. I took it all in and felt a little sadness and nostalgia as goose bumps rippled up and down my body. I reached the house and slowly made the right hand turn into the driveway.

As the front wheels of my car hit the bump at the end of the driveway, the radio, which I had previously tuned out, started playing a new song that captivated me from the first note. I had never heard the song before in my life and I was barely aware of the artist, Daughtry. I never watched American Idol. I parked the car at the end of the driveway, turned off the engine and turned the music up. The house was dark and seemed so empty and lonely. Not even the porch lights were on. As the words of the song "Home" began, I suddenly felt a chill. It was as if this song was written for me, for this moment. I knew that it was no coincidence that this song began at the very moment I arrived.

> *"I'm staring out into the night.*
>
> *Trying to hide the pain.*
>
> *I'm going to the place where love*
>
> *And feeling good don't ever cost a thing.*
>
> *And the pain you feel's a different kind of pain."*

I couldn't believe how poignant the words and melody

were and how appropriate it was for this moment. I will never forget it or how it felt. It brought a familiar feeling and I knew it once again, just like on the mountain that night that I wasn't alone. I felt so filled with contentment and satisfaction as the words continued to ring in my head.

"I'm going home.

Back to the place where I belong.

Where your love has always been enough for me.

I'm not running from, no I think you got me all

wrong. I don't regret this life I chose for me."

"But these places and these faces are getting old

So I'm going home.

I'm going home...."

I just sat there in the driveway listening to the most beautiful song I had ever heard in my life. I stared at the house and visualized all of the years and all of the moments that made us a family and made this our home. As I wiped the corners of my eyes with the sleeve of my shirt, I started to notice something.

Just beyond the house, at the edge of the woods. Something was moving. First in the distance and then slowly moving closer and closer. There they were. Hundreds, if not thousands of lightning bugs coming down through the trees and glowing bright, blinking on and off like the lights of a Christmas tree in perfect streaks of yellow just as they had done all of those years ago. I immediately remembered my wish to Mom as she took her last breath. I had prayed for a sign. I had prayed for one more lightning bug in the trees. And here they were. Just for me. I finally had my sign.

I lost my breath at first when I saw them. I got the overwhelming sense that everything was going to be all right. I don't know a better way to describe it.

Everything will be all right. I was not alone.

It was magical and unforgettable. As the song continued on, I realized they were here. I could feel both of them. Mom and Dad were here with me. I couldn't hear them or see them, but I could feel them. It felt warm and familiar like I had put on a blanket from my childhood.

My skin was covered in mounds of goose bumps and I felt an extreme peace. To me, this was it. This was the last chapter of this story and the first chapter of the rest of my life.

The proof I had been seeking my entire life was here in front of me and for the first time, I knew it to be true.

The culmination of my journey and all that I experienced up to this point was the existential proof of an existence beyond our life that I had been searching for. I can't understand exactly what that existence is yet but I also know that I am not supposed to. I don't need to either. I have faith that it is there.

As the song played, I could see all of the moments we had at this place playing through my mind. It was as if I was at a drive-in movie. I could see every Christmas, every Steelers game and all of our birthdays. I saw myself cutting the grass while dad manned the grill. I laughed as I recalled the day my front tooth got knocked out by a hockey stick, boy did mom go berserk.

I could see everything all at once, as if it was a part of me and I was a part of it. I remember how the trees would sway in a storm and the way it would smell after a rain. I remember the happy times and of course, Dad's finger points out on the street.

The memories just kept coming, flooding my mind like a film on fast forward. Family. Love. Memories.

I was here for the last time and I could feel them here with me watching the same great show I was, with a smile across their faces. And for the first time in my life, it all made sense to me.

"My mind found peace.
My soul found hope.
My heart found a home."

-Lyrics from When Mercy Found Me
by Rhett Walker Band

AFTERWORD

It has been almost six years since I said my last goodbye to my Dad on that dark and brutally hot evening in Salzburg. To this day I continue to reflect on what my experiences in the last moments of his life had taught me. I still miss my Dad. But I no longer question what happened or try to explain it. What happened was real. What he saw was real. What I felt was real.

I set out to write a book about losing my Dad and how much he meant to me. I wanted the world, and in particular my children to know what an amazing guy he was and to understand what he meant to me.

In the end, I now realize that this book was as much about me and my journey as it was about my Dad. I could have never arrived where I am today were it not for him. I find myself so thankful and humbled that even in death he was still acting as my father and showing me the way, even if he wasn't aware of it at the time. His dramatic ending and everything that came with it showed me proof of something beyond our physical existence and brought something that I had never really had. It brought me faith.

I often think back to the last real conversation I had with Dad. It was our "Tuesdays with Morrie" moment. And he was right. The things that matter most are love and the special moments that we get to share with the ones we love the most.

As Eckhart Tolle teaches us, a happy life is a series of

happy moments. This, in a straightforward way defines with an absolute clarity what my "one thing" is. It is the moments we should behold, cherish, revel in and hold onto and never let go. The great moments that make life worth living can and will be surrounded by some not-so-great moments and sometimes real pain too. But we can't let it cloud us or distract us from seeking, creating and living for the moments with the ones you love.

It is the first time you hold your little baby in your arms and weep tears of pure love and joy.

It is the first time you fall in love, when the touch of a hand sends waves of electricity through you.

It is the perfect feeling of peace when holding your lover or watching the sunset over the mountains or feeling your bare feet in the surf.

It is holidays together as a family, a simple walk through the park and watching your children grow over the years.

Ultimately, it is all about love and sharing that love and connection with those closest to us through our lives. It sounds so simple but it's easy to get lost.

I lost my way and got caught up in all of the meaningless details of life and actually stopped living it the way I wanted to.

Through the experience of Dad's death, and what I was personally able to witness and experience, I connected to my one thing and it has changed me forever.

The ability to filter out the noise of life and stay focused on finding, creating, celebrating and cherishing those moments comes and goes and sometimes remains as fleeting to me as it is to most everyone.

As I reflect back on this experience, I feel that I now understand that and embrace the best moments of my life with my Dad. Embracing the present moments and understanding them for what is important in life, makes me feel fulfilled and connected to those I love and even helps me to stay connected to those who have passed on.

I don't pretend to know the secret to life and I don't pretend to know the answers to the mysteries of the universe, but I also don't feel like I need to. I don't feel that I am supposed to "yet" and I am OK with that.

My lifelong struggle to find meaning and answers to unanswerable questions has been replaced with an understanding that there are things I am not meant to know and that I don't have to know. Dad couldn't hear the angel "yet" because he wasn't ready to or wasn't meant to. We are not meant to know everything until our journey is complete.

What I do know with conviction after this experience is that there is something beyond our existence. It is loving, benevolent, whole and eternal and it is a part of all of us. It was there for me all along. I just didn't know how to connect to it. I was able to connect to it through this experience and now I want to connect to it as often as I can. It is not easy. But now, as I embrace the moments of my life, I feel just that much closer to it and it is real and fulfilling in ways that I couldn't have imagined before.

I went from barely breathing to finding meaning. I found what I have been looking for throughout the balance of my life. My "one thing" was right in front of me the entire time.

But now I know it's there and that in itself comforts me and gives me the sense that everything is going to be all right. Our existence and our purpose for being here and what we are meant to get out of this life is bigger than whatever we are feeling from time to time or whatever we struggle through.

The meaning of life is different for each person, and you have to figure it out for yourself. But for me, I have found it and I will try with everything I have to keep my promise to my Dad to embrace it and protect it. I will cherish every moment I have with the ones I love. I will live for those moments.

Since Dad died, from time to time I have moments when the world quiets and the chaos of life pauses ever so briefly. It is in those times that I find myself back on that mountain in Salzburg in the rain or by his bedside in our final moments or in the driveway in Harrisburg surrounded by lightning bugs. I can still feel it like it was yesterday and I can feel the loving presence that I felt in those moments. It's still there. Now I know it will always be there. In these moments I can feel Dad watching over me. And I can just picture him standing there giving me the finger point, and I know deep in my heart and without any doubts what it means.

And it feels great.

Cause these are the days' worth living
And these are the years we're given
And these are the moments
These are the times
Let's make the best out of our lives"

-Lyrics from Our Lives by The Calling

Please visit www.Barely-Breathing.com to share your thoughts or experiences with others who have lost a loved one, had experiences with death-bed visions or who tirelessly search for faith and meaning.

Made in the USA
Monee, IL
21 October 2022

16316559R00108